Faculty Perspectives on Vocational Training in South Africa

The Cape Peninsula University of Technology (CPUT) is one of nine Universities of Technology established by the South African government in 2005 with a focus on vocational training. This book presents faculty experiences of CPUT's innovative, work-integrated learning and teaching model, as well as findings from practice-based research being done in the institution. The purpose of this volume is to be a resource for other institutions in South Africa that wish to try similar strategies, as well as to trigger a community of practice with vocationally oriented institutions outside of South Africa.

Eunice N. Ivala is an associate professor and coordinator of the Educational Technology Unit at Cape Peninsula University of Technology in Cape Town, South Africa.

Chaunda L. Scott is an associate professor in the Department of Organizational Leadership and the diversity and inclusion specialist for the Office of the Dean in the School of Education and Human Services at Oakland University, Rochester, Michigan, USA.

Faculty Perspectives on Vocational Training in South Africa

Lessons and Innovations From the Cape Peninsula University of Technology

**Edited by
Eunice N. Ivala and
Chaunda L. Scott**

Routledge
Taylor & Francis Group

LONDON AND NEW YORK

First published 2019 by Routledge

2 Park Square, Milton Park, Abingdon, Oxfordshire OX14 4RN

52 Vanderbilt Avenue, New York, NY 10017

Routledge is an imprint of the Taylor & Francis Group, an informa business

First issued in paperback 2020

Copyright © 2019 Taylor & Francis

The right of Chaunda L. Scott and Eunice N. Ivala to be identified as editors of this work has been asserted by them in accordance with sections 77 and 78 of the Copyright, Designs and Patents Act 1988.

All rights reserved. No part of this book may be reprinted or reproduced or utilised in any form or by any electronic, mechanical, or other means, now known or hereafter invented, including photocopying and recording, or in any information storage or retrieval system, without permission in writing from the publishers.

Notice:
Product or corporate names may be trademarks or registered trademarks, and are used only for identification and explanation without intent to infringe.

Library of Congress Cataloguing-in-Publication Data
Names: Ivala, Eunice N., editor. | Scott, Chaunda L., editor.
Title: Faculty perspectives on vocational training in South Africa : lessons and innovations from the Cape Peninsula University of Technology / By Eunice N. Ivala and Chaunda L. Scott.
Description: New York : Routledge, [2019] | Includes bibliographical references.
Identifiers: LCCN 2018059229 | ISBN 9781138499683 (hardback) | ISBN 9781351014311 (ebk)
Subjects: LCSH: Education, Higher—Aims and objectives—South Africa. | Cape Peninsula University of Technology—Curricula. | Technology—Study and teaching (Higher)—South Africa.
Classification: LCC LA1538 .F33 2019 | DDC 378.00968—dc23
LC record available at https://lccn.loc.gov/2018059229

ISBN: 978-1-138-49968-3 (hbk)
ISBN: 978-0-367-67022-1 (pbk)

Typeset in Times New Roman
by Apex CoVantage, LLC

We dedicate this volume to the legacy of Nelson Mandela and Cape Peninsula University of Technology academic faculty, staff and students, past, present and future.

Contents

Foreword

Higher education transformation in South Africa is an area of much contemporary debate. There is a vibrant synergy of creative strategies to engage a wide repertoire of issues that include curriculum, teaching and learning, technology, decolonisation, redress and access of marginalised students based on race and class. The transformation discourse has been dominated by access to higher education, however, more recent debates included strategies for improving success, higher levels of participation with emancipatory pedagogies, the innovative use of technology to enhance teaching and calls for radical change with regard to institutional culture.

The 2015 #FeesMustFall and #RhodesMustFall movements heralded the decolonial turn in South African higher education, adding new impetus to the transformation agenda, with greater emphasis on curriculum change and the intersectionality of race, class, inequality and social justice. The critical move from the global South to disrupt the master narrative by engaging with alternate knowledge frameworks and disrupting particular epistemic gridlocks on theory and content choices emphasised the decolonial turn. There is a strong focus on three critical frames of the decolonial turn in the scholarship from the global south: power, knowledge and being, as these three domains reinstate the colonial space. These frames are essential to ensure critical engagement with crucial issues in higher education and to disrupt the colonial paradigm at universities, especially with regard to curriculum and institutional culture.

Transformation is not its own goal; the goal is an improved, just and equitable society. Both colonialism and apartheid have negatively affected the nature of educational provision and order in South Africa. Almost every level of education (both schools and tertiary institutions) were cast in a racial mould: educational budget provisions, the structure of educational bureaucracies, the composition of staff and students, the kind of curriculum followed and the ethos prevalent in universities. Transforming higher education should therefore address changes in various levels. This requires a contestation and

repositioning of the past educational order, a redefinition of the culture prevalent in universities and a fundamental shift from a racist, undemocratic and
authoritarian institutional culture.

South African academics need to explore new ways of learning and teaching to break the cycle of the dominant stance of knowledge consumption and
the training and production of skilled acolytes who are good at banking education and poor at cognition and higher thinking skills. Our strategies should
point toward ways of producing students that can generate new knowledge
and are able to critique the current knowledge frameworks in their specific
disciplines and to imagine new ways of approaching 21st-century problems.
In fact, the true test of our relevance and worth as academics is the extent our
students are able to transcend the current knowledge paradigms and are able
to respond in a creative and groundbreaking manner to a future which cannot
be imagined. This places great expectations and responsibilities on scholars in
higher education. To ensure that our students are able to reimagine the future,
we need to reflect on our own engagement with knowledge and the strategies
we may use to engage with a generation whose visual literacy and savvy with
technology are leaps ahead of our traditional ways of doing things.

A cursory glance of curricula in the humanities reveals outmoded notions
of what to teach, outdated ideas of how to teach and most importantly, epistemological perspectives that ignore our specific African context and the fact
that we are African academics teaching African students. Indigenous forms
of knowledge, culture and skills used by working-class and rural people in
a modernising society continue to be submerged and denigrated. Inherent in
all this is the mimicry of Western knowledge traditions as the only reliable
and valuable content. Spivak refers to it as worlding (1999)—how colonised
spaces have normalised western knowledge as sovereign. Hence, our transformation agenda demands great courage to disrupt epistemological gridlocks, particularly theories from the North. Transformed ways of teaching
and learning are integral to the current call for a transformed and decolonised
higher education landscape.

The continuities with apartheid and colonisation in South African society have not been fully addressed within the neoliberal and marketisation
approaches in higher education governance and culture. Historically, South
Africa has been characterised in all aspects of life by enormous disparities
in power and accessibility to education. This has not only been the case in
a racial sense but also in terms of gender, class, region, age and urban–rural
relationships. The radical transformation of higher education has to engage
deeply with the nature of the continuities with apartheid and how this should
be disrupted. Curriculum was integral to the colonisation and apartheid
agenda, and this has not been addressed nor acknowledged in significant
ways. In my interaction with colleagues who may be termed *traditionalists*

because of their resistance to the transformation of curricula in their discipline, the underlying concern is the almost total oblivion of how black students view institutions as a culture of inequality, silence and coercion. There is something profoundly wrong when, for instance, syllabuses designed to meet the needs of colonialism and apartheid should continue well into the liberation era (Mbembe, 2016). It is evident that the nexus between colonisation and curricula in higher education needs to be strongly foregrounded in transformation debates.

Colonisation not only involved physical, military and economic invasion but was also accompanied and justified by attempts to export Western knowledge. Western universities were heavily implicated in this process. The key features of Western knowledge include a focus on the individual, racial and gender hierarchies; rationality; privileging written over oral texts; linear constructions of time and space; and a binary either/or logic (Mbembe, 2016). In the process of knowledge production, the North was the location of knowledge and theory, whereas the South functioned as a giant laboratory. An important consequence of this Northern dominance of knowledge production is the value we place in the West and our limited appreciation of indigenous knowledge from Africa, what Ngugi wa Thiong'o (1986) calls the "colonisation of the mind." Essentially, colonisation seeks to capture the self-doubt and dependency on the North. The age of imperialism has led to a "spirit of helplessness" in the global South, to the point where we regard only Western writings and theories as proper sources. The coloniality of power from Western categories of thought is so pervasive that it is difficult to extricate ourselves from it, and therefore epistemic delinking is advocated. De-linking entails epistemic disobedience (Santos, 2007) rather than the constant search for newer concepts to examine power, racism and the like. In epistemic delinking, the locus of enunciation is relocated in the subaltern spaces, a shifting from Western understandings and bringing forward other principles of knowledge and understandings. It seeks to move away from strict disciplinarity to transdisciplinarity, and to a disruption of the territorial hold on curriculum, by building theories without or beyond disciplines. We need to rethink how the academe has constituted disciplines and the division of knowledge into boxes like economics, anthropology, history, philosophy, literary criticism and sociology, among others. More appropriately, transdisciplinarity will hopefully provide solutions to the complex problems faced in the global South. A curriculum that transcends borders will draw from different disciplines, adding a richer texture to the engagement with knowledge, an important principle that we should consider in the current call for curriculum transformation in higher education.

If *curriculum* is understood as the formal knowledge that makes up certain categories and disciplinary divisions set together with particular classroom practices and principles which are underpinned by a set of ideologies and discourses, then intellectualization of the curriculum means interrogating the formulation of what constitutes curriculum—*Who is influential in curriculum development, what is the influence and what is the outcome of such curricula?* (Mbembe, 2016). Transformation not only calls for an intellectualization of the curriculum but also for an alertness to neoliberal influences. Market-related governance is visible in the terminology of university speak as its intellectual longings have been replaced by performance management, funding and grants, research units, productions units, international rankings and the like. Important components of the knowledge industry like social impact, the nature of learning, radical pedagogies and the value of alternate/ "other" knowledge paradigms seems to be located at the periphery within the neoliberal institutional structure that places more emphases on marketisation, funding and fiscal priorities than on knowledge generation.

Epistemological marginalisation is visible in colonised spaces that view the canon as legitimate knowledge. Santos (2007) terms this exclusion of the other as epistemicide. The disruptive impulse would intervene on repetitive mainstream narratives and promote critical engagement with marginalised discourses. Disruption does not simply mean changing the positionalities of actors in particular sets of power relations; it also means creating the conditions in which agency and voice can emerge. The focus on content as curriculum and curriculum transfer of powerful knowledge has an implicit *a priori* theoretical position in relation to the social context. Its position is to view the social and bigger questions around politics, power, race and class, as subjective externals to the curriculum. The key shortcoming with this position is that the social context is pushed to the margins. Soudien (2006) rightly argues that social logics of curriculum should be the theoretical fulcrum and emphasises an openness to the knowledge of subordinate people. Curriculum disruption would benefit from a balanced approach towards the social, that is undoing of our racist legacy via the curriculum together with an internally compelling imperative for powerful knowledge. There is a bifurcation of the ontological (being) and the epistemological (knowing). The further danger towards this view of curriculum is that the subjectivity of academics is clouded by the so-called objectivity stance; in other words, the racialised neo-liberal hegemonic discourse dominates under the guise of objectivity. It is simplistic to separate social discourses from knowledge discourses in South Africa, given the context of inequality and a racialised society. The danger of separating the knowledge from the social is that academics offer a functionalist view of the curriculum as a corrective measure to fill in the gaps of powerful knowledge in the student. This view is further reinforced with the academic stance taken against Black students as underprepared and low achievers in benchmark tests.

Efforts to embrace a truly egalitarian society and eliminate racism, the ideological cornerstone of apartheid policy, need to be recognised and acknowledged in any discussion of educational reform post-1994. There are remarkable continuities between apartheid-era management principles and current trends in higher education with its hierarchies of power, autocratic ways of administering academic departments and erosion of collegiality among academics (often stuck within racial paradigms). Rather than arguing whether racial practices or the significance of race has declined or changed in higher education, the focus should be on assessing whether transformation has occurred in the racial structure of throughput; that is have we moved beyond the low rates of graduation of Black students (currently at 9%)? The student resistance during #FeesMustFall highlighted the socio-economic struggles of students given the rising levels of poverty in South Africa. The transformation agenda of higher education has to take serious account of the psychosocial contexts, well-being, welfare and struggles of poor students. Poor Black youth from working-class backgrounds are direct victims of the low-quality public education system that has not prepared them adequately for tertiary education. This accounts for the racial structure of throughput and achievement both at undergraduate and postgraduate level and further reinforces racial inequality.

Bourdieu's (1990) notions of social and cultural capital are attributes used in universities to reward students who have high cultural capital (middle-class students) and to punish those who have low social capital (poor students). Higher education has to engage deeply with student resistance and not repeat the knee-jerk reaction during the 2015 #RhodesMustFall crisis that crippled institutions. Essential to the transformation agenda is the voice and agency of students in an authentic manner. Listening to the voices of students, our key stakeholders in higher education, would have prevented the militarisation of our institutions, damage to property and deaths of students during the recent revolt. We need to engage with what has provoked the anger of students, particularly for the curriculum reform agenda, the ways students see Fanon's theorising around the wretched of the earth and Biko's black consciousness as crucial to address the epistemological gaps in curricula. And finally, we should engage with class far more vigorously and honestly. There is a substantial discrepancy between what students without basic resources deserve and what they actually receive in universities (Chetty, 2014). A truly transformed higher education would not reproduce race and class inequities, would halt the drive of working-class students toward academic ignorance and civic alienation and would enhance the journey of students toward high scholastic achievement, academic mastery and democracy.

Dr. Rajendra Chetty
Professor of Education
University of the Western Cape

References

Bourdieu, P. (1990). *In other words: Essays towards a reflexive sociology*. Cambridge: Harvard University Press.

Chetty, R. (2014). Class dismissed? Youth resistance and the politics of race and class in South African education. *Critical Arts, 28*(1), 88–102.

Mbembe, A. J. (2016). Decolonizing the university: New directions. *Arts & Humanities in Higher Education, 15*(1), 29–45.

Santos, B. de S. (2007). Beyond abyssal thinking: From global lines to ecologies of knowledge. *Review, 30*(1), 45–89.

Soudien, C. (2006). Thwarted access: Race and class. In *A review of the state of education in South Africa ten years after 1994, final report*. South African Democratic Teachers Union. Johannesburg: Centre for education policy and development.

Spivak, G. C. (1999). *A critique of postcolonial reason*. Boston: Harvard University Press.

Wa Thiong'o, N. (1986). *Decolonizing the mind: The politics of language in African literature*. Nairobi, Kenya: Heinemann Education Publishing Ltd.

Preface

Over the past two decades in post-apartheid South Africa, research remains scant regarding what kinds of higher education transformation strategies have been developed, utilized, worked, and needed at universities of technology to assist in moving them beyond their post-apartheid state of being from the perspective of South African academic faculty. This Focus Book gives voice to South African academic faculty members and affiliated scholars at Cape Peninsula University of Technology (CUPT) located in Cape Town, South Africa, which is the only technological university in the Western Cape and the largest one in terms of enrollment in the region. In this focus book, academics share their insights regarding the kinds of unique transformation strategies that are working as well as needed at CPUT. The information in this volume will be useful to scholars globally who are interested in learning from CPUT academic faculty members and scholars affiliated with CPUT about the policies and practices used, as well as the ones needed to drive higher education transformation at CPUT in post-apartheid South Africa.

Chapter 1, the introduction chapter, begins by introducing and summarizing the benchmarks established by the Republic of South Africa that have been used to guide the transformation in higher education since apartheid ended in 1994. These benchmarks are *The Education White Paper 3: A Programme for the Transformation of Higher Education* (Department of Education, 1997), *Transformation and Restructuring: A New Institutional Landscape for Higher Education* (Minister of Education, 2002) and, most recently, the *Policy Framework for the Realization of Social Inclusion in the Post School Education and Training System* (Minister of Higher Education and Training, 2016). In the next section of this chapter, a brief history of CPUT located in Cape Town, South Africa, is presented along with a discussion on how these benchmarks have guided higher education transformation at CPUT. Thus, the aim of chapter serves to provide the context for the following chapters written by CPUT scholars and scholars affiliated with CPUT.

Chapter 2 highlights a blended programme aimed at working adult students learning implemented at CPUT, as a part-time Baccalaureus Technologiae (BTech) in Architectural Technology. This programme, offered in collaboration with an industry partner, is delivered as an office-based, online and on-campus blocked learning and teaching model. This chapter presents the blended programme, explores through flexible learning principles, learning design strategies for improvement and broader application at the institution and beyond.

Chapter 3 asserts that higher education institutions (HEIs) in South Africa have recently experienced significant shifts, as the collective student body called for radical transformation in academic discourse and practice. The call for change could be witnessed in the 2015 and 2016 student protests that challenged the academic status quo at various HEIs across South Africa, resulting in discussions and debates and, in some cases, division with regard to the call for decolonized and free education. The uprising revealed that although there have been significant shifts in what was once considered a fragmented and structurally racialized system to a moderately more unified higher education system in SA, transformation has remained elusive.

Chapter 4 argues that globally, education is regarded as indispensable for the growth and development of a country. Education is also viewed as allowing individuals to become productive citizens who can compete in the global marketplace. Nonetheless, for this to be possible, the principle of equal access to opportunities has to be realized. In a country such as South Africa, with a history of the apartheid system, the challenge to provide all citizens with opportunities for access and success in education has been marred by a lack of equity. This chapter presents two of the most pressing transformation challenges in the South African higher education system. These challenges are juxtaposed with initiatives, policies and practices that have been initiated by government and universities to improve the experiences of students, particularly those from previously disadvantaged backgrounds. The chapter ends by suggesting that more still needs to be done to ensure that diversity and transformation becomes a reality in the South African higher education system.

Chapter 5 highlights a digital storytelling classroom activity in a senior-phase education course at a large university of technology in Cape Town, South Africa. Teacher education students spent eight weeks participating in a digital storytelling unit meant to teach them how to communicate with diverse learners across varied sociocultural and historical contexts. Framed by literature stemming from the turn of higher education after the onset of democracy in South Africa, the sustainability of the digital storytelling project was questioned with an interest in, if the students carried this knowledge from the university classroom into their teaching practices.

Chapter 6 presents staff experiences of the merger and transformation processes and outcomes, along with the lessons learned at CPUT, in order to allow the merged institution to measure the outcomes of the merger and lessons learned and to plan ways for improving on whatever merger goals have not been achieved. Furthermore, understanding the outcomes of the mergers and the lessons learned will enable institutions to design relevant interventions to advance the transformation of institutions and to address any concerns that may have arisen as a result of the mergers.

Chapter 7 discusses that despite the increased local and global call for critical thinking and critical citizenship as an essential skill and graduate attribute for students, the teaching in the current Extended Curriculum Programme at CPUT, in general, and in the Architectural Technology and Interior Design Department, in particular, falls short in this matter because of curriculum requirements, workload, time constraints and the need to work toward industry expectations. This chapter focuses on critical thinking and critical citizenship—which aims at the production of socially conscious graduates that will become the thinkers and leaders of tomorrow.

Chapter 8 details a theoretical approach developed for curriculum transformation project driven from the Centre for Higher Education and Development at a University of Technology. This project is funded through University Capacity Development Grant and seeks to respond towards calls for decolonization of South African higher education following unprecedented student protests that engulfed South African higher education in the 2015, 2016 and 2017 academic years, respectively. Central to the student protests was unequivocal call for the free and decolonized higher education. In this project, the authors intend to use their knowledge and expertise in collaboration with actors interested in the project in fighting against a global colonial white system that continues to marginalize black people in South Africa, in the broader African continent and globally (in particular, the global South), to create transformative learning opportunities and facilitate epistemic justice for all.

References

Department of Education. (1997, July). *Education White Paper 3: A Programme for the Transformation of Higher Education*. Pretoria, South Africa. Retrieved from www.gov.za/sites/www.gov.za/files/18207_gen1196_0.pdf

Minister of Education. (2002, June). *Transformation and Restructuring: A New Institutional Landscape for Higher Education*. Retrieved from www.dhet.gov.za/Reports%20Doc%20Library/New%20Institutional%20landscape%20for%20Higher%20Education%20in%20South%20Africa.pdf

Minister of Education. (2016, December). *Policy Framework for the Realization of Social Inclusion in the Post School Education and Training System*. Retrieved from www.dhet.gov.za/SiteAssets/Latest%20News/2017/January/Gazetted-Policy-Framework-for-the-Realisation-of-Social-Inclusion-in-PSET-No40496-Notice-no-1560.pdf

Acknowledgments

First, we would like to thank the Cape Peninsula University of Technology chapter authors in this volume and the academic reviewers from the Republic of South Africa and the United States for their time, and expertise that they dedicated to this book project. I, Dr. Eunice N. Ivala, am thankful to Dr. Chaunda L. Scott, who came up with the idea for this Focus Book project when she was a Fulbright Specialist Scholar in 2015 at Cape Peninsula of Technology in Cape Town, South Africa, and for leading this book project to fruition. Next, we would like to thank Dr. Rajendra Chetty for contributing the foreword to this volume. Last, but not least, we want to thank Matthew Friberg, Education Editor at Routledge, for the feedback and guidance he provided us that helped to make this book project possible.

Introduction

Presently, limited research exists on the current status of transformation in the higher education in post-apartheid South Africa, from the perspective of South African academic faculty. Utilizing case studies, the objective of this co-edited anthology is to highlight South African faculty perspectives from Cape Peninsula University of Technology (CPUT), located in Cape Town, South Africa. The volume uncovers their views on the current status of transformation of higher education South Africa, along with an understanding of the strategies CPUT faculty and affiliated faculty are utilizing and or developing to move beyond their post-apartheid state of being to:

1. produce graduates at the undergraduate, master's and doctorate levels with the knowledge, skills and abilities to contribute successfully in industry, the community and globally;
2. guarantee fair access to qualified individuals in management, staffing and student recruitment from all cultural backgrounds;
3. create and advance diverse and multicultural teaching practices and programming;
4. build and advance support for quality research and teaching that benefits the demographic composition of South African academics and students and the needs of the South African multicultural society;
5. build new institutional identities of merged and non-merged higher education institutions in order to rise above preceding apartheid injustices; and
6. gather recommendations from the South Africa academic community on how to further advance the transformation of higher education institutions in post-apartheid South Africa.

The background data for this co-edited volume is derived from benchmarks established by the Republic of South Africa as highlighted in the following documents: *The Education White Paper 3: A Programme for the Transformation of Higher Education* (Department of Education, 1997), *Transformation and Restructuring: A New Institutional Landscape for Higher Education document* (Minister of Education, 2002), and most recently the *Policy Framework for the Realization of Social Inclusion in the Post School Education and Training System* (Minister of Higher Education, 2016). Building on these three documents, six research questions were formulated, which also serve as the six chapter themes for this volume:

1.   What strategies are being utilized or could be utilized at CPUT in Cape Town, South Africa, to produce graduates at the undergraduate, master's and doctorate levels with the knowledge, skills and abilities to contribute successfully in the industry, the community and globally?
2.   What strategies are utilized or could be utilized at CPUT in Cape Town, South Africa, to guarantee fair access to qualified individuals in management, staffing and student recruitment from all cultural backgrounds?
3.   What approaches are being utilized or could be utilized at CPUT in Cape Town, South Africa, to create and advance diverse and multicultural teaching practices and programming?
4.   What strategies have been introduced or could be introduced at CPUT in Cape Town, South Africa, to create and advance support for quality research and teaching that benefits the demographic composition of South African academics and students and the needs of the South African multicultural society?
5.   What new institutional identities have been developed or could be developed by a merged university like CPUT in Cape Town, South Africa, to rise above preceding apartheid injustices?
6.   What additional policies, practices and initiatives would be beneficial in further advancing the transformation of higher education at CPUT and broadly at institutions of higher education throughout South Africa?

The preceding six themes served to guide the chapter authors in this volume in shedding light on the current status of the transformation of higher education at CPUT and higher institutions throughout South Africa. Recommendations were also shared by the authors in this volume regarding how to further advance transformation efforts at CPUT and at higher education institutions throughout South Africa.

Co-editors

Eunice N. Ivala is an Associate Professor and Coordinator of Educational Technology at Cape Peninsula University of Technology, Cape Town, South Africa.

Chaunda L. Scott is an Associate Professor of Organizational Leadership and Diversity and Inclusion Specialist at Oakland University in Rochester, Michigan, USA.

References

Department of Education. (1997, July). *Education White Paper 3: A Programme for the Transformation of Higher Education*. Pretoria, South Africa. Retrieved from www.gov.za/sites/www.gov.za/files/18207_gen1196_0.pdf

Minister of Education. (2002). *Transformation and Restructuring: A New Institutional Landscape from Higher Education*. Retrieved from www.dhet.gov.za/Reports%20 Doc%20Library/New%20Institutional%20landscape%20for%20 Higher%20Education %20in%20South%20Africa.pdf

Minister of Education. (2016). *Policy Framework for the Realization of Social Inclusion in the Post School Education and Training System*. Retrieved from www.dhet. gov.za/SiteAssets/Latest%20News/2017/January/Gazetted-Policy-Framework-for-the-Realisation-of-Social-Inclusion-in-PSET-No40496-Notice-no-1560.pdf

1 Cape Peninsula University of Technology

A Discussion on the Transformation of Higher Education in Post-Apartheid South Africa Through the Lens of Governance, Reconstruction and Social Inclusion

Eunice N. Ivala and Chaunda L. Scott

Introduction

> Education is the most powerful weapon you can use to change the world.
> —Nelson Mandela (The Borgen Project, 2018)

Much has been written on the topic of transforming the South African (SA) higher education (HE) system over the past several decades. Yet, research remains limited regarding what transformation strategies have been effective, ineffective or needed from the perspective of South African academic staff members working at universities of technology in post-apartheid SA. Particularly as it relates to assisting the SA's HE system in moving beyond its post-apartheid state of being. This chapter begins by introducing and summarizing the benchmarks established by the Republic of SA that have been used to guide the transformation in HE since apartheid ended in 1994. These benchmarks are the *Education White Paper 3: A Programme for the Transformation of Higher Education* (Department of Education, 1997), *Transformation and Restructuring: A New Institutional Landscape for Higher Education* (Ministry of Education, 2002) and, most recently, the *Policy Framework for the Realization of Social Inclusion in the Post School Education and Training System* (Minister of Higher Education and Training, 2016). In the next section of this chapter, a brief history on Cape Peninsula University of Technology (CPUT), located in Cape Town, SA, is presented along with a discussion on how the benchmark established by the Republic of SA have guided transformation at CPUT. Thus, the aim of the chapter serves to provide the context for the following chapters written by CPUT scholars and affiliated scholars.

**Transformation Policy Frameworks
for Post-Apartheid HE in SA**

1. The **Education White Paper 3: A Programme for
the Transformation of Higher Education**

SA's transition from apartheid and minority rule to democracy required that all existing practices, institutions and values are viewed anew and rethought in terms of their fitness for purpose in the new era. Higher education plays a pivotal role in the social, cultural and economic development of modern societies. As a democracy for more than 20 years, SA is still redressing past inequalities and efforts are made to transform the HE system to serve a new social order, to meet pressing national needs and to respond to new realities and opportunities. The former Department of Education (DoE) released the *Education White Paper 3: A Programme of Transformation for Higher Education* in July 1997. This *White Paper 3* outlines a comprehensive set of initiatives for the transformation of HE through the development of a single coordinated system with new planning, governing and funding arrangements. As stated in the white paper, all higher education institutions (HEIs) should implement these initiatives in their work. In this white paper, the transformation of HE is explained as the eradication all forms of discrimination; the promotion of equity of access and fair chances of success for all; the advancement of redress of inequalities; meeting, through its teaching, learning and research programmes and national development needs, including the economy's high-skilled employment needs; supporting democratic ethos and a culture of human rights through education programmes and practices conducive to critical discourse and creative thinking, cultural tolerance and a commitment to a humane, non-racist and non-sexist social order; and contributing to the advancement of all forms of knowledge and scholarship and upholding rigorous standards of academic quality.

2. **Transformation and Restructuring: A New Institutional
Landscape for Higher Education**

The institutionalization of apartheid in every facet of South African life after the apartheid government came to power in 1948 had a significant impact on education. Separate education departments, governed by specific legislation and fragmented along racial lines, reinforced the divisions in the education system (Malherbe, 1977). Educational provision at the end of the apartheid era in 1994 was fragmented, and based on ethnic separation and discrimination. After the democratic election in 1994, it became evident that there was a need for a new democratic education system that ensured equality in all aspects of education (Sayed, 2000). According to Makgoba (2008, p. 1), the new government inherited:

> a HE system whereby the leadership was unable to provide the vision needed to meet the knowledge and scholarship challenges of HE in the context of national transformation, globalization and a development state . . . the sector suffered an identity crisis, the effects of poor human capital production levels, fragmentation along race lines, a lack of sustainability and a structural incapacity to meet the rigorous challenges of reconstruction and development.

Structurally, fundamental and long-standing problems existed, which included the geographical location of institutions, which was based on ideological and political considerations rather than rational and coherent planning. This resulted in fragmentation and unnecessary duplication and the continued and increasing fragmentation of the system. Education did not work in a coordinated way—there were limited successful cooperative initiatives and programmes between institutions; major inefficiencies related to student throughput rates (low throughput rates), graduation (low graduation rates), student dropouts (a large number of students drop out), student repetition and the retention of failing students and unit costs across the system; skewed patterns of distribution of students in the various fields of study—science, engineering and technology; business and commerce; and the humanities and education—with a greater concentration of students in the humanities and education fields relative to other fields; the distribution of students in the various levels and fields of study, at certain institutions, was skewed in terms of race and gender; academic and administrative staff (in many fields and disciplines and at different levels) also displayed poor patterns of race and gender representation and distribution; most institutions had extremely low research outputs; and even those institutions with a higher ratio of research outputs relative to other institutions had uneven levels of outputs (CHE Shape and Size Task Team, 2000). These structural characteristics undermined the cost-effectiveness, efficiency and equity. They created a kind of differentiation that is neither desirable, sustainable or equitable in a developing democracy.

The post-apartheid HE institutions were also faced with immediate or contextual problems which included institutional responses that exacerbated the inherited fragmentation and incoherence of the system and the inefficient and ineffective utilization of resources; competition between public institutions around programme offerings and student enrollments, which overshadowed cooperation and led toward homogeneity and sameness in an environment of declining enrollment; a decline in student enrollments within public HE sector compounded by a decline in retention rate of students from the first to succeeding years of study, and the overall participation rate for the age group 20–24 remained static and was estimated for 1999 at 15%; the possible inability of several institutions to continue to fund their activities because of the relationship between enrollments and funding, as well as their inability to attract more diverse sources of funding, the inability of many students to pay fees and the institutions' lack of capacity to collect fees have resulted in increases in students debts; concerns around quality, the effective protection of learners and possible adverse effects on the public HE systems by the increase in private HEIs who were at that time inadequately regulated in terms of registration, accreditation and quality assurance; fragile governance capacity (council, management, administration and students) in many of the institutions; inadequate senior and middle management capacities within the system; the rapid incorporation of information and communication technologies within HE; and the inadequate information systems, especially in relation to finance matters. As a result, many institutions lacked the capacity to provide and process basic data and information (CHE Shape and Size Task Team, 2000).

As a result of the preceding challenges, the inherited HE system was not effectively responding to the new needs of the country and there was a need to restructure the HE system. In December 2002, the then minister of education, Professor Kader Asmal, announced that the cabinet had approved the final proposal for the restructuring of the institutional landscape of HE in SA. The restructuring of HE was in line with the constitution of SA, which emphasizes the new democratic government's commitment to restoring the human rights of all marginalized groups, and the bill of rights, which entrenches the rights of all South Africans to basic education and access to educational institutions regardless of race, gender, sexual orientation, disability, religion, culture or language (RSA, 1996); the National Plan for Higher Education (Ministry of Education, 2001) stressed the need to ensure the "fitness for purpose" of the South African HE system (Makgoba, 2008); and the *Education White Paper 3: A Programme for the Transformation for Higher Education* 1997, advanced equity and redress, quality, development, effectiveness and efficiency (CHE Shape and Size Task Team, 2000).

The overall objective of the restructuring of the HE landscape was the development of a HE system that delivers effectively and efficiently and is based on equity, quality and excellence; responsiveness; and good governance and management (CHE Shape and Size Task Team, 2000). The *White Paper 3* called for a coherent, coordinated and integrated national HE system that is simultaneously differentiated and characterized by diversity. Differentiation was used to refer to the social and educational mandates of institutions, and diversity was used with reference to the specific institutional missions—which were said should be varied. The purpose of differentiation and diversity was to ensure a range of institutions, institutional programmes and capabilities appropriate to national needs.

The envisaged outcomes of the restructuring were a much more clearly specified range of institutional mandates that encouraged diversity through explicit, clear and coherent institution-specific missions in their pursuit of production of knowledge and graduates; a clearer and more targeted set of objectives for the investment of resources to strengthen quality and equity; a prospect of increasing overall participation levels in HE and ways of addressing the challenge of equity of access; a more focused framework for innovation in teaching and learning, research and in community service through a concentration of resources and attention on niche areas; the provision for and encouragement of different modes of teaching, learning and assessment and the establishment of possibilities and limitations of different modes of delivery for different institutional focuses; and the acknowledgment of a framework for competition, as well as collaboration, within the public sector as well as between the public and the private HE providers as competition within a properly regulated system enhances quality (CHE Shape and Size Task Team, 2000).

As a result of the restructuring process, the number of universities in SA was cut from 36 to 23 through incorporations and mergers. However, the government in 2014/2015 established 3 more universities to bring the total of public universities to 26. Public universities in SA are divided into three types: traditional universities, which offer theoretically oriented university degrees; universities of technology ("technikons"), which offer vocational-oriented certificates, diplomas and degrees; and comprehensive universities, which offer a combination of both types of qualification. Thus, the country has 9 universities of technology; 6 comprehensive universities; and 11 traditional universities. These universities accommodate in excess of 1 million students, with plans by the government to add 500,000 to that total by 2030 (see https://businesstech.co.za/news/general/101412/here-are-south-africas-26-universitieshttps://businesstech.co.za/news/general/101412/here-are-south-africas-26-universities/).

3. The Policy Framework for the Realization of Social Inclusion in the Post School Education and Training System

The policy framework was developed in 2016 in an effort to understand social inclusion in the Post-School Education and Training (PSET) system and to ensure the implementation of social inclusion in all forms of PSET institutions (public universities, HE colleges, university colleges, Technical and Vocational Education and Training [TVET] colleges and private universities). Additionally, the policy is intended to help the Department of Higher Education and Training (DHET), and HE and training institutions in implementing and reporting on elements of social inclusion. Furthermore, the policy will assist DHET in ensuring that the transformation priorities of the department are taken into account at all PSET institutions. The framework will also assist the DHET in strengthening relationships with other government departments dealing with issues of social cohesion, ensuring that there is synergy and shared understanding as far as the implementation of social inclusion is concerned and addressing a major challenge facing the (PSET) system—the lack of an integrated framework defining the road map to a socially inclusive PSET system that is in line with the values of the South African constitution.

The framework situates the PSET system within the universal human rights discourse, which recognizes social inclusion as a concept that embraces the entire humanity and cuts across all the factors that divide human beings. In this discourse, social cohesion is said to recognize the fact that all human beings, regardless of national boundaries of states, socioeconomic background, age, disability, ethnic or racial origin, religion and any other form of belief are entitled to human dignity and should be protected by the State. Thus, the policy framework was developed in alignment with the Universal Declaration of Human Rights proclaimed by the United Nations General Assembly in Paris on 10 December 1948 (General Assembly resolution 217 A), which sets a common standard of achievements for all peoples and all nations. The Universal Declaration of Human Rights spells out, for the first time, that fundamental human rights should be universally acknowledged and protected. In its preamble, it recognizes the inherent dignity and the equal and inalienable rights of all people as the foundation of freedom, justice and peace in the world; the South African Bill of Rights embedded in the Constitution of the Republic of SA (RSA, 1996). The bill of rights acknowledges the rights of all people in SA and affirms the democratic values of human dignity, equality and freedom.

The policy framework recognizes the values underpinned in the preamble of the constitution and which are also restated in the *Manifesto on Values, Education and Democracy*, as published by the DoE in 2001. These values are democracy, non-racism and non-sexism, (Ubuntu) human dignity and social justice, accountability, respect, reconciliation and unity in diversity. The policy framework is also based on the transformation priorities of the DHET as stated in its strategic plans. These are race, class, gender, disability, language, age, HIV and AIDS, geography and citizenship in its broader sense.

The policy framework compliments other DHET and various government departments existing policies and legislation that address social inclusion issues in PSET (Minister of Higher Education and Training, 2016). The DHET hopes to create a conducive environment for social inclusion in post-school education and training, an environment that will ensure that social inclusion-related policies and legislation in institutions are developed, implemented and monitored. The policy framework also complements various international and national policies to enhance human dignity and affirm the bill of rights embedded in the Constitution of the Republic of SA. The DHET and institutions reporting to it are expected to align their implementation strategies and long-term plans with these international conventions and declarations. In this regard, the DHET is obliged to contribute to periodical country reports and to work collaboratively with other departments addressing issues of social inclusion.

The policy framework situates social inclusion in the constitution, and delineates the principles of social inclusion as constitutional democracy; human rights and equality; non-racialism, non-tribalism and non-sexism; unity in diversity; inclusivity and social justice; redress and transformation; intergroup and community cooperation; social solidarity; civic responsibility; and national consciousness. It further locates social inclusion within the South African context and argues that social inclusion is characterized by a set of shared values, norms, visions and goals that foster bonds of belonging. These bonds cut across racial, ethnic, national and religious identities. Hence, social inclusion refers to interconnectedness among members of the human race and can be defined in clear terms as a sense of human solidarity. The framework notes that social inclusion goes beyond the concept of social cohesion and nation building and comprises all people, even those who do not share similar value systems, territories and histories.

Even though a lot has been achieved in attaining social inclusion in SA, including the instituting of a solid policy and legislative environment, major challenges still exist. The *Ministerial Report on Transformation and Social Cohesion and the Elimination of Discrimination in SA's Public HEIs* (Department of Education, 2008) revealed that there was still racism and other forms of discrimination in South African public HEIs. Other identified challenges were a lack of transformation in areas such as gender and disability and the representation of other racial groups in academic positions. The report also highlighted the need not only to promote diversity in the student population but also to ensure that the academic staff composition is equally diverse and institutional cultures of exclusion are transformed. The report additionally showed that HEIs do not have a shared understanding of "transformation" and "social cohesion."

In order to realize social inclusion in the PSET system, the policy framework states five strategic themes: eradication of poverty and social exclusion in the system by mobilization all PSET institutions and stakeholders in the sector toward common social inclusion objectives, common indicators to measure progress in the achievement of social inclusion, the development of evidence-based progress reports indicating performance against national action plans on social inclusion, mutual learning and exchange on social inclusion in the PSET system and social inclusion assessment in the form of annual reports on progress of social inclusion in PSET. According to the policy frameworks, for PSET system to work toward achieving social inclusion, institutions should focus on the following:

• Governance—governing structures of institutions should be representative, freedom of association and freedom of expression as articulated in Chapter 2 of the Constitution should be observed and the training of council members in social inclusion dimensions is critical as these structures are crucial in the development and implementation of progressive institutional policies.

• Democratic representation of staff and students—democratic representation for both staff and students cannot be divorced from the broader debate of social inclusion, access and transformation. The policy framework supports staff development, the creation of posts and mentorship as part of institutional plans and departmental initiatives such as the new Generation of Academics Programme (nGAP), which encompasses both historically advantaged and disadvantaged HEs. It further suggests that institutions should have clear transformation-supporting policies and guidelines with regard to teaching and learning and staff promotion and clear indicators for teaching, learning and research. Additionally, university councils should establish functional employment equity processes and procedures and monitor and report on employment equity trends in terms of the Employment Equity Act and that employment equity should be part of vice-chancellors' employment contracts.

• Improving access to previously disadvantaged students—government aims for addressing financial support for students in institutions through increased National Student Financial Aid Scheme (NSFAS) financial allocations and new management systems, as well as the recent focus on the "missing middle" (refers to students above NSFAS threshold but for whom university education is unaffordable), as most Black students entering HE come from poor and middle class households.

• Addressing the needs of students and staff with disabilities—the framework supports the Ministerial Statements on Disability Funding and the norm that all infrastructural programmes have to address disability issues. It notes that most universities have progressed significantly in developing disability units, building needed infrastructure to support staff and students with disabilities and implementing disability policies.

• Dialogue forums—establishment of dialogue forums should be encouraged and supported in institutions as they nurture a culture of debate and democratic participation in public affairs.

- Gender equity—according to The Human Sciences Research Council policy brief (July 2014), the quality of educational experiences for both male and female students remains poor in SA, and thus, there was a need for priority assistance for women in the PSET system. This assistance must be formalized in institutional policies and should be grounded on applicable national legislation. Gender-equity policies and targets should be put in place in all institutions and be part of PSET institutions' transformation reports, and targets should not only be limited to the number of women admitted as students or employed by institutions but should also address their occupation of leadership positions, participation in postgraduate studies and their participation and success rate in previously male-dominated programmes such as engineering and political sciences.

- Health care and HIV/AIDS—institutions must prioritize the establishment of health centers and student support services, in order to promote healthy lifestyles on and off campus, assist staff and students in health-related issues and, specifically, conduct an HIV and AIDS information and awareness campaign.

- Student accommodation—institutions should have placement policies that will be centrally monitored by the residence office of each institution and the framework pleas for the abolition of any form of racial segregation and discrimination in student residences. The policy calls for the banning of initiation ceremonies and activities, "irrespective of whether an activity causes bodily harm or not" as these activities and ceremonies could be used as a cover to promote racial bigotry in institutions and thus threaten social cohesion. It further calls for institutional employment equity policies to be applied to residence employees in order to avoid the perpetuation of the ethnic or racial composition of residence staff.

With the understanding that: social inclusion and transformation cannot be separated, government fiscal budget constraints and the recommendation that integrated planning and implementation within current budgets will need to be used to attain the goals of this policy framework, the fact that social inclusion implementation in institutions was to begin in 2018/2019, that a DHET monitoring and evaluation report on social inclusion is absent (as the policy states that this evaluation will be done in 2019/2020, to evaluate the scope and effectiveness of institutional policies), that HEIs do not have a shared understanding of transformation and social inclusion and that the implementation of transformation and social inclusion will not be the same for all institutional types, the subsequent section presents CPUT's efforts toward transformation and social inclusion.

Transformation of HE and Social Inclusion at the CPUT

As part of the restructuring of the HE in SA, CPUT was constituted on 1 January 2005, as result of a merger between the Cape Technikon (formerly for White students but opened its doors for other races in 1987) and the Peninsula Technikon (formerly for Colored students but its opened doors for other races in 1987). CPUT, as a university of technology, is vocationally oriented, awarding higher certificates, diplomas and degrees in technology, and has some postgraduate and research capacity (www.ieasa.studysa.org/ resources/Study_SA/Facts_Figures_section.pdf). The mission of CPUT is to build a university that is highly efficient, sustainable and environmentally conscious; to be known for the high quality of its teaching and learning and relevance of its curriculum; to create a vibrant and well-resourced living and learning environment for its students; and to enhance and develop the quality and effectiveness of its research and knowledge production (www.cput.ac.za/ about/vision). The university currently serves 32,000 students and has several campuses and service points and offers more than 70 programs (degrees, diplomas and certificates). The university has 1,000 permanent academic staff members.

Toward the transformation and social inclusion agenda, CPUT has a comprehensive institutional transformation strategy (CPUT, 2013) and a transformation, social cohesion and diversity charter (see www.cput.ac.za/storage/ services/transformation/transformation_charter.pdf). The institution also has policies which support transformation, namely, an employment equity policy, a recruitment and selection policy, a policy for people with disabilities, a policy for the employment of foreign nationals, an ad hominem promotion policy for academic staff, a performance management policy, a student initiation policy, a quality assurance policy, a student admissions policy, an academic planning framework, a sexual harassment policy, a language policy, a Khula policy and a recognition for prior learning policy.

The implementation of the transformation policy is centralized in the vice-chancellor's office, while at the same time faculties/units/departments and individuals are given space to construct and implement transformation initiatives in their specific contexts. The institution has a transformation unit tasked with overseeing transformation and social inclusion initiatives. Institutional and faculty transformation committees exist. Toward equity in enrollments using equity by group from 2007 to 2011 (CPUT, 2013), most of the students in the institution were African, followed by Colored, White and a very small number of Indian students. About 80 percent of the students receive funding from NASFAS, meaning they come from poor households. In 2011, the university had 175 students with disabilities, 58 of whom were foreign nationals, and 5 staff members with disabilities (CPUT, 2013). A disability unit is in place to assist students and staff with disabilities, and some of the infrastructures in the university have been modified to ensure access for people with disabilities. The university promotes multilingualism and has a language unit. Through the work of the language unit, there is an institutional language policy, a multilingual online glossary of difficulty terminologies from subjects from different disciplines is in place and there is the use of sign language during graduation ceremonies.

Attention has been paid to staff development and transformation by introducing intervention measures such as nGAP, which encompasses both historically advantaged and disadvantaged HEIs. In 2011, the university had 12 Khula candidates, 2 per faculty. The preceding initiatives have the potential of changing the academic landscape of SA in all disciplines as young black South Africans will be able to start the journey of becoming academic researchers, thus addressing the anomalies identified by the *Education White Paper 3: A Programme for Transformation of Higher Education*. The university has units for continuous staff development in teaching and learning.

The university recognizes The DHET's "Calendar of Significant Days," which ensures staff and student participation in activities that promote social cohesion, community service and inclusion. The institution actively observe Human Rights Day (21 March), Freedom Day (27 April), Youth Day (16 June), Mandela Day (18 July), Women's Day (7 August) and Heritage Day (24 September) to celebrate unity in diversity and the birth of democracy and freedom in SA, and Africa Day on 25 May is celebrated to emphasize SA's place on the African continent, though this day is not a public holiday in the country.

Despite the earlier achievements by CPUT, documentation on institutional achievements as far as transformation is concerned is scanty, and scholarly research is limited regarding what transformation strategies have been effective, ineffective or needed from the perspective of South African academic staff members working at universities of technology in post-apartheid SA and as it specifically relates to assisting SA's HE system in moving beyond its post-apartheid state of being. This Focus Book, titled *Faculty Perspectives on Transformation of Vocational Training in Post-Apartheid South Africa: Lessons and Innovations from Cape Peninsula University of Technology*, is a result of a research collaboration that Dr. Chaunda L. Scott led as a Fulbright Specialist Scholar in the Republic of SA. In 2015, Dr. Scott received a prestigious Fulbright Specialist Scholar award at CPUT located in Cape Town, SA. As a Fulbright Specialist Scholar at CPUT, she had an awesome opportunity as an associate professor of organizational leadership and diversity and an inclusion specialist in the School of Education and Human Services at

Oakland University in Rochester, Michigan, US, to provide diversity education workshops to academic faculty and staff members at CPUT's Fundani Center for Higher Education Development, and engaged in diversity education research. The products that were produced from the diversity education research she engaged in with Dr. Eunice Ivala, an associate professor and coordinator of educational technology at CPUT, resulted in two Routledge Focus Books, in which this volume is one of those publications. The second Focus Book that Drs. Scott and Ivala co-edited is titled *Transformation of Higher Education Institutions in Post-Apartheid South Africa.* The aim of these two publications is to provide an opportunity for South African academic faculty members at CPUT and academic faculty representing various universities throughout the Republic of SA to share their perspectives on the kinds of strategies being currently utilized and needed to transform SA's HE system beyond its post-apartheid state of being.

References

The Borgen Project. (2018). *Top nine Mandela quotes about education.* Retrieved from https://borgenproject.org/nelson-mandela-about-education/

Cape Peninsula University of Technology. (2013). *Comprehensive transformation strategy: Towards a great University.* Retrieved from www.cput.ac.za/storage/services/transformation/transformation_strategy.pdf

Council on Higher Education Size and Shape Task Team. (2000). *Towards a higher education Landscape: meeting the equity, quality and social development imperatives of South Africa in the 21st Century.* Council on Higher Education, Pretoria.

Department of Education. (1997, July). *Education white paper 3: A programme for the transformation of higher education.* Pretoria, South Africa. Retrieved from www.gov.za/sites/www.gov.za/files/18207_gen1196_0.pdf

Department of Education. (2008). *Report of the Ministerial Committee on Transformation and Social Cohesion and the Elimination of Discrimination in Public Higher Education Institutions.* Retrieved from https://www.ukzn.ac.za/wp-content/miscFiles/publications/ReportonHEandTransformation.pdf

Makgoba, M. W. (2008). *In practice: Engaging with leaders in higher education.* Leadership Foundation for Higher Education, issue No. 16. Retrieved from http://ifhe.ac.uk

Malherbe, E. G. (1977). *Education in South Africa.* Vol. 2: 1923–1975. Cape Town: Juta.

Ministry of Education. (2001). *Draft National Plan for Higher Education in South Africa.* Retrieved from http://www.dhet.gov.za/HED%20Policies/National%20Plan%20on%20Higher%20Education.pdf

Minister of Education. (2002). *Transformation and restructuring: A new institutional landscape from higher education.* Retrieved from www.dhet.gov.za/Reports%20Doc%20Library/New%20Institutional%20landscape%20for%20 Higher%20Education%20in%20South%20Africa.pdf

Minister of Higher Education and Training. (2016). *Policy framework for the realization of social inclusion in the post school education and training system.* Retrieved from www.dhet.gov.za/SiteAssets/Latest%20News/2017/January/Gazetted-Policy-Framework-for-the-Realisation-of-Social-Inclusion-in-PSET-No40496-Notice-no-1560.pdf

Republic of South Africa. (1996). *Constitution of the republic of South Africa*. Pretoria: Government Printer.

Sayed, Y. (2000). *Post-apartheid educational transformation: Policy concerns and approaches*. Paper presented at EAKA Conference. New Orleans.

Theme 1

What strategies are being utilized or could be utilized at Cape Peninsula University of Technology in Cape Town, South Africa, to produce graduates at the undergraduate, master's and doctorate levels with the knowledge, skills and abilities to contribute successfully in the industry, the community and globally?

2   Flexible Learning Provision for Architecture in South Africa

Lessons Learnt From an Industry-University Collaboration

Jolanda Morkel and Johannes Cronjé

Introduction

It is often overlooked that many students

> either work in the formal or informal sector; care for the old or the young; are parents and/or surrogate parents to siblings; live and learn with disability or chronic illness; are returning or interrupting students; and live and learn in formal or informal housing environments. 'This non-traditional student life' has become the norm.
>
> (Jones & Walters, 2015, pp. 62, 63)

Yet, few universities have succeeded to "open (their) doors (Walters, Witbooi, & Abrahams, 2015) in the spirit of lifelong learning to workers and professionals in pursuit of multi-skilling and reskilling, and adult learners whose access to higher education had been thwarted in the past" (Jones & Walters, 2015, p. 62). Traditional offerings through full-time and part-time options must be re-examined to "enable both working and non-working students' equal access to and success in undergraduate studies" (Jones & Walters, 2015, p. 64).

The first blended programme aimed at working adult students, that comprises a significant online component, implemented at the Cape Peninsula University of Technology (CPUT), is the part-time Baccalaureus Technologiae (BTech) in Architectural Technology. This programme, offered in collaboration with an industry partner, is delivered as an office-based, online and on-campus blocked learning and teaching model. This chapter presents the blended programme, explored through flexible learning principles, towards the formulation of design strategies for improvement and broader application at the institution and beyond.

Architectural Education in South Africa

The architectural profession in South Africa is regulated by the South African Council for the Architectural Profession (SACAP). It registers architectural professionals at the levels of draughtsperson, technologist, senior architectural technologist and architect. Despite various attempts by universities to support previously disadvantaged individuals, demographic transformation of the profession remains slow since 1994. Most of the previously disadvantaged professionals are still registered at the "lower levels," that is at draughtsperson or technologist levels (Poulsen & Morkel, 2016).

Architectural education is costly through its reliance on personalised learning and intensive design tutor support. Learning is project-, problem- and inquiry-based (Ellmers & Foley, 2007; De la Harpe et al., 2009; Kuhn, 2001; Maher & Simoff, 2000) and happens mainly in the design studio that has provided the signature pedagogy (Shulman, 2005) for almost 100 years. Theoretical subjects equip students with base knowledge to formulate innovative solutions to complex problems while design tutors help them to develop design expertise through regular feedback on their work. Such feedback is provided in graphic and verbal formats during a learning activity known as the design critique (crit), tutorial or seminar (Blair, 2006; Lymer, 2009; Morkel, 2017).

Rapidly changing workplace demands, growing economic pressure, increasing student numbers, challenges with student readiness and access, diversification of the student body, pervasive use of social media and information and communication technology (Ivala & Gachago, 2012), uncertainty about the future role of the university and a call for the decolonisation of higher education (Ryan & Tilbury, 2013) demand a relook at the architectural education landscape in South Africa and the world. The one-size-fits-all educational model that caters to a small number of privileged individuals has become obsolete (Morkel, 2013; Morkel, 2016a; Morkel, 2016b; Morkel, 2016c; Poulsen & Morkel, 2016).

Blended Part-Time Programme

It is in response to these challenges that the blended part-time BTech in Architectural Technology progamme was developed at CPUT. The resident part-time BTech programmes at both pre-merger institutions had been abandoned, due to unsatisfactory results and misalignment with the full-time equivalent (Van Graan, 2016).

Based on the lessons learnt from the interventions piloted in the undergraduate studio, especially those tested in the experiential learning (second) year of the National Diploma programme, the first author and a colleague (drawing on expertise by the second author) designed a blended part-time BTech programme in 2012. Due to a range of institutional obstacles, its implementation was delayed until 2014 when Open Architecture, the non-profit unit of the South African Institute of Architects (SAIA) agreed to collaborate with CPUT to implement this non-traditional mode of an existing architectural university curriculum, thereby providing alternative perspectives for working adult learners.

The student intake on the part-time BTech ranges between 22 and 34 per year. Working students come from the all over South Africa, that is Cape Town, Johannesburg, Pretoria, East London, Port Elizabeth, Durban and Polokwane, as well as neighbouring countries Namibia, Zimbabwe and Mauritius. Of the first cohort admitted in 2014, 13 students graduated in 2015, showing a 60% pass rate—seven with Previously Disadvantaged Individuals' (PDI) backgrounds. Since then, between 15 and 20 students graduate each year.

Methodology

This chapter documents design strategies that emerged from the first three years of implementation, based on participant observation and student, tutor and mentor feedback on the course. These include important perspectives by prominent "players" that Jane Kettle (2013, p. 69) refers to in her work on flexible learning for working adult learners as the university, the student and the employer.

The broad parameters of flexibility in learning and teaching practice formulated by the University of Southern Queensland, Australia, and adopted by the flexible learning project at the University of the Western Cape (UWC; Jones & Walters, 2015) are used to frame these perspectives, namely

- **flexible curriculum design**, including flexible forms of assessment which consider different learning preferences of students;
- **flexible admissions criteria**, including mechanisms such as the recognition of prior learning (RPL) and credit accumulation and transfer;
- **flexible delivery**, including distance, online, on campus and a mix of these modes of delivery, as well as accelerated or decelerated options; and
- **flexible support systems** and services that cater to all students and staff, including those with disabilities, allowing for universal access to learning.

—added by Jones and Walters (2015)

Two publicly available YouTube videos and four online surveys conducted via Google Forms, gathered over a three-year period, contain perspectives representing the university, the student and the employer (Kettle, 2013, p. 69). These were thematically analysed according to the flexible learning framework presented earlier.

The first YouTube video, "2015: Open Architecture—The Student Experience" (duration 5:18), contains a range of student voices (ST 1–7). The video was commissioned by Open Architecture to show prospective students what they can expect from the student experience. It was produced by Epitome, whose photographer spent an afternoon on campus during one of the block sessions. The brief was to elicit student responses on successes and challenges and to suggest any hints or advice for new applicants. Students were approached randomly, and the videographer selected the most telling material to produce the video, with the students' permission. The video is available on YouTube at www.youtube.com/watch?v=W0t8M6BkM_M.

The second video is "2016: CIfA CPD: Open & Alternative Architectural Education" (duration 1:27:05). It is a screencast of a live CPD presentation at the local Voluntary Association (VA), the Cape Institute for Architecture (CIfA), that was also offered as an online event to showcase the blended programme to the architectural professional community. The recording is available online at www.youtube.com/watch?v=vbCTg89KLxU. The session included presentations by representatives of the professional body, the university, the student body, mentors and educators. The mentor–student pair was selected as an example of a successful mentor–mentee collaboration.

Finally, four surveys provide more student and employer/ mentor perspectives as follows:

> 2015: Year 1 (10) and Year 2 (10) students (i–xx), 50% of each respective group
> 2015: Employer/mentor (1–13) feedback (13 out of 40 responded)
> 2016: Employer/ mentor (a–t) feedback (20 out of 40 responded)
> 2017: Year 1 students (A–I) feedback on Step Up programme (9 out of 21 responded)

Flexible Learning

Flexible learning aims to "expand the range of opportunities for individuals to access and succeed in higher education (HE) at a time, pace and place to meet their needs, which traditional modes of study do not support" (Hammersley, Tallantyre, & Le Cornu, 2013, p. 5). It goes so far as to challenge the full-time–part-time binary system in its entirety (Jones & Walters, 2015).

It accommodates accelerated and decelerated programmes through part-time studies, allowing for credit accumulation and transfer (CAT) and access via recognition of prior learning (RPL). It can support a variable pace of study within a programme's overall deadlines and allows "learners to 'roll on/roll off' ('stop in/stop out')" (Jones & Walters, 2015, p. 64). Furthermore, it supports work-based learning with employer engagement, employer responsive course provision and the accreditation of in-company training programmes. Aided by technology, it can accommodate off-campus learning to enable the flexibility of learning across geographical boundaries, at convenient times, and enriching the learning experience.

The Blended Part-Time BTech Architectural Technology as a Flexible Learning Model and a Flexible Curriculum Design

The part-time BTech adopted the same curriculum as the professionally accredited full-time programme. The ultimate test of a student's competence in architecture is the summative pin-up portfolio review (Blair, 2006; Lymer, 2009; Webster, 2005). It is a public assessment conducted with a student presenting his or her work (drawings and models) and responding to questions posed by the tutors/examiners and moderators. To ensure fairness to the students and parity between the full-time and part-time programmes, the same portfolio review formats were used, and the same external moderators were appointed for both programmes. Since the programme follows the full-time curriculum, it is not currently characterised by flexible curriculum design.

Flexible Admissions Criteria

The minimum requirement for the blended part-time BTech programme is a National Diploma or similar approved. In addition, a minimum of one year's work experience in architectural practice is compulsory, a range of selection instruments are employed. In 2016, 12 students were admitted through a process of RPL (Poulsen & Morkel, 2016), and the first RPL candidates graduated in 2017. Although the demand for access via RPL is growing, there is currently no mechanism by which RPL applicants can improve their chances of being selected. Experienced architecture professionals are typically competent in technical and management areas and less so in the domains of theory and design. To achieve more flexible admission strategies in the future, online and blended professionally mandatory Continuing Professional Development (CPD) and short courses could be employed to provide bridging in these areas (Morkel, 2016c; Van Graan, 2016).

Flexible Delivery

The part-time programme is a decelerated model. The one-year full-time curriculum (120 credits) is offered over two years part-time. In the first year, 66 credits are completed and 54 in the second year. Design and construction projects are guided by a timeframe, with biweekly synchronous webinars.

Theoretical subjects are self-paced, and learners may organise their own time in-between preset milestones, which is in alignment with Ryan and Tilbury's (2013) call for decolonised HE experience.

The course comprises three components that, together, promote interactive learning. These components are office-based mentorship, online engagement and on-campus blocks (Poulsen & Morkel, 2016). On the success of the programme, one lecturer has this to say:

> I'm amazed and surprised at the depth of engagement and the level of the knowledge that the students have built up in a very short period of time, and it suggests to me that although there were many questions asked . . . and . . . the whole idea of architectural education being done online as opposed to the traditional studio, that it's time that we looked at the development of other forms of delivery . . .
>
> (Van Graan, 2014)

The success of the programme relied on the supportive environment provided in the architectural practice, mentor support and the student work experience.

Office-Based

The student must be employed in an architectural practice where a SACAP registered professional senior architectural technologist or architect can mentor her for the full duration of her studies. The relationship between the university/Open Architecture and the student and mentor is guided by a memorandum of agreement (MoA) signed by the relevant parties at the start of each year. The office is meant to provide the student with a stimulating real-world environment and opportunity for feedback and advice on the university projects that are completed alongside her office commitments:

> So, my mom couldn't pay for all of us, so I had to go work and it's very difficult because architecture was never offered part-time, like it is now . . .
>
> (ST4, 2015)

Employers/ mentors value the benefits that the student brings to the office:

> [T]here is a great deal of improvement in his design mentality and communication skills; there is a notable improvement in his thinking process.
>
> (Mentor h)

And they acknowledge what the office as a learning context, in turn, contributes to the learning:

I think the influence of working in a practice has been very beneficial to the Open Architecture design project . . .

(Mentor 5)

However, the tension that's evident in many of the employers/mentors' responses affirms Kettle's (2013, p. 67) observation that "there are inherent tensions between the motivations of universities and of workplaces regarding flexibility, among other issues." We concur with Abrahams (2014), who shows that the relationships between students and their employers are often mixed. Conflict often results from different forms of knowledge, competing agendas, practical arrangements for learners and workplaces and the autonomy of the university, of the employer and of the learner (Kettle, 2013):

The clash of deadlines between his office tasks and university tasks would occasionally result in difficulties.

(Mentor 3)

Although the mentors support the students' studying in principle, some are unwilling to offer the two days per week as specified by the MoA. Still some practices are keen to contribute to the greater good of the profession:

If you live and practice in South Africa, it is essential to support the growth of learning for all. And your system provides the perfect platform— well done!

(Mentor 1)

Some employers feel that government incentives and rewards might be helpful:

I think making the government aware of our contributions to education would probably be a big help. Currently the system in place does not reward professionals accordingly as we are forced to discount our fees and compete against each other for work in order to survive.

(Mentor 5)

In this study, learning in its setting is work-related rather than work-based because it happens "alongside and external to the curriculum" (Kettle, 2013, p. 23). In work-based learning provision, content is created by the learner from work activity and any prior learning is agreed in a learning contract. To better utilise office time for learning, future strategies to assess office work for credit through closer university–employer/practice collaboration, and the accreditation of in-company training programmes, should be investigated, as suggested by one of the mentors:

Perhaps some consideration should be given to more integrated tasks and assessments. The course could call for projects from participating practices.

(Mentor 3)

To achieve this, closer collaboration with workplaces are required, possibly distinguishing between different kinds of practices and their potential contribution, as well as the training of office staff.

Online

The online and on-campus block interactions are designed to limit time out of the office to a minimum whilst still achieving the required number of notional hours:

The use of communication technology and remote access for students reduces the amount of time spent out of office.

(Mentor 3)

Through online engagement, the office-based and on-campus learning is optimised. Synchronous and asynchronous, formal and informal engagements are facilitated. Email correspondence is reserved for private and personal correspondence only, which means that all students have access to all the learning exchanges (Poulsen & Morkel, 2016):

I do it via my cellphone—it is easy; it doesn't matter what device you have, as long as you can connect on to the internet.

(Student 9)

The Learner Management System (LMS) provides a calendar, announcements, submission of and feedback on student work and lecture recordings. Students' Design Journals present an opportunity for asynchronous interaction via graphics and text and weekly webinars for (recorded) synchronous engagement using images and audio. Although the use of Facebook for informal learning conversation is not encouraged by all employers, students find it convenient and easy to use:

Everybody is on [F]acebook and you get alerts as things happen.

(Student ii)

The use of technology to enable flexible learning and teaching and the pedagogical implications that arise from this are emphasised by Kettle (2013, p. 68). Because students are studying from the workplace, they have access to infrastructure like printers, Internet and so on. However, although employer-support expectations are guided by the MoA, some students are better supported than others. In future, pre-registration interaction with the employers could help to clarify any misunderstandings about the study demands and to avoid digital exclusion of those already marginalised (Appiah & Cronjé, 2013, 2014).

On-Campus Blocks

Three compulsory one-week-long block release programmes are offered on campus in Cape Town every year (Poulsen & Morkel, 2016). They provide opportunity for concentrated content input by lecturers and invited guest experts, group work, project feedback sessions and support programmes—see "Step Up" programme discussed later. Block periods are often planned to coincide with recess periods when on-campus venues are readily available. Although on-campus periods are kept to a minimum to satisfy official requirements for contact programmes, they are understandably unpopular with employers/mentors:

> Block weeks [are] a big interruption. Maybe shorter periods, every 2nd month, for say 2/3 days, instead of a week almost every quarter.
>
> (Mentor j)

However, block sessions provide an opportunity to build a community of learners, facilitate group work and accommodate peer to peer feedback:

> It's useful because it gives us (students) broader sense of engagement, also as colleagues it's useful to see how other peers are doing and you can always ask one-on-one question be it to the lecturers or among ourselves.
>
> (Student v)

Extended Programme

An extended track was introduced this year in response to requests for more time and to address the drop-out rate:

> We suggest that a course like this needs to be more flexible in allowing students to develop at their own pace and in sync with their own lives and commitments.
>
> (Mentor e)

However, of the three students who transferred to this track during the second term in 2017, two students dropped out completely soon after anyway. It could be that they were simply too far behind already or that there were other factors hindering their success. It appears that simply extending the time is not enough to ensure success. In future, this problem may be addressed by improved communication with the employers and applicants prior to registration, introducing different augmented alternatives, based on the specific circumstances of the student and his or her employer, and an improved model through which the full-time/part-time divide is eradicated. There cannot be a "one-size-fits-all" approach but, as Kettle (2013) argues, systematic communications will be required between workplaces and universities to enable a truly flexible pedagogy to support working students.

Flexible Support Systems and Services

This aspect of the flexible learning framework, added by Jones and Walters (2015), addresses important strategies to support academic staff and students, including those with disabilities, to ensure academic success.

Student Support

The programme relies on a partnership between highly motivated staff and involved employers and mentors to support student learning:

> The fact that you offered such great support to Rafeeq, and that often our conversations were concurrent with the ones that you were having with him.
>
> (Mentor 1)

Most mentors are positive about mutually beneficial relationships and developmental benefits offered to mentor and mentee alike:

> The process allows you as a professional to keep on learning new things and revising and updating your professional experience . . .
>
> (Mentor 4)

The role of the mentor to complement the tutor role, is important for student success.

> [I]t was amazing that in that what the lecturers were saying and what my mentors were saying, it coincided . . .
>
> (Chafeker, 2016)

Although not unusual for architectural studies, the relatively high drop-out rate is alarming. It could be ascribed to financial, work-related and/or personal problems rather than inability (Poulsen & Morkel, 2016). Time management, self-regulation and communication are important skills that students require to balance work, family and studies; to negotiate the perceptions of employers; and to put mechanisms in place to free up time to fully participate in the programme.

> One mustn't under estimate how much time the course does take . . .
>
> (Mentor 6)

> Students must be encouraged to communicate clearly with their mentors regarding time planning.
>
> (Mentor 5)

The three-day programme was condensed into a one-day Step Up programme designed and presented by Carol Pearce (2017) and adjusted for this context in collaboration with the first author is offered to the Year 1 group during the mid-year block. The programme draws on Zimmerman's theory of self-regulation as "the degree to which students are metacognitively, motivationally, and behaviourally active participants in their own learning processes" (2008, p. 167).

It comprises a theoretical introduction, followed by three sessions, that are Life-Style Management & Understanding the Adaptive Process, Mindset Intervention; Expand Self-Awareness & Enhance Self-Regulation; and "Build Effective Practice"—Personal Change Management Plan (Pearce, 2017). In the feedback, most students indicated that they found it valuable:

> Prioritising whatever little time I have, appropriate allocation of that time and learning to set boundaries with those around me . . . I think that's exactly what most of us need. We know what we need to do but just don't seem to be getting it right because we don't have the how pegged.
>
> (Student H)

But they suggest that it needs to be extended:

> More time should be allocated to this course. The Step Up program holds vital sets of tools to navigate this part time study programme successfully.
>
> (Student G)

The Step Up programme introduces a language of self-awareness and professional development that staff and students can use to address obstacles to learning.

Staff Support

Kettle (2013) suggests that all staff appointed to work in flexible learning contexts need support and training to develop suitable pedagogies. They also need the "confidence, understandings and opportunities to develop practices to make any such learning effective" (p 28). The different pedagogies associated with this approach are only likely to be effective and flexible if the right personnel are engaged to deploy them (Kettle, 2013, p. 28).

Programme Support

We agree with Kettle (2013, p. 31) that policies, procedures and business models must enable educational alliances of employers and universities to enable flexible learning and teaching for access and success of working students. Flexible learning cannot take place within an inflexible infrastructure (Outram, 2009, cited in Kettle, 2013, p. 74). It is dependent on "other parts of the institution, including its IT systems, quality processes and general administration as well as political will" (p. 28). Only once the infrastructure is in place, and the systems are robust, can flexibility be accommodated. It requires resourceful leadership to effect these changes (Johnston, 1997).

Conclusion

In this chapter, we presented data from the two-year blended part-time BTech degree programme as a flexible learning and teaching model in terms of flexible curriculum design, flexible admissions criteria, flexible delivery and flexible support systems and services (Jones & Walters, 2015), the latter focusing on student support. We drew on university, employer and student perspectives gathered from video material and online surveys.

Although flexible delivery is achieved through blended learning, successfully employing technology for rich and engaging learning experiences brought to working students in remote settings, the work-based learning modality is not yet optimised. More flexible approaches may be achieved through employer-responsive pedagogy to "manage learner demands and expectation in a fast-changing world of work" (Kettle, 2013, p. 25).

The curriculum remains aligned with the current full-time programme and guided by professional accreditation. It therefore not yet allows flexible forms of assessment that considers different learning preferences of students. In the future, the next iteration of the learning design should aim to move beyond the current practices of the full-time/part-time binary modes.

Admissions criteria are flexible to an extent, insofar as it allows for RPL. However, RPL and other applicants are not yet supported through portfolio, bridging or short-course provision or credit accumulation and transfer. These strategies can be explored in the future, especially in view of the lessons learnt from implementing blended learning strategies. A more flexible model should also be able to scale the programme to accommodate a larger number of students at any given time.

Findings demonstrate how staff (design tutors), mentors and specialised consultants (Step Up programme) can promote flexibility through student-centred facilitation and support. However, staff and programme support systems and services at the university have not yet adequately shifted to support a flexible programme of this nature.

Through further research, continuous reflective practice, redesign and implementation, hopefully a change process that can "shift pockets of enthusiasm of flexible learning and teaching towards a coherent, institutionalised outcome" (Johnston, 1997, p. 74) can be achieved.

References

Appiah, E., & Cronjé, J. (2013). ICT, ideation pedagogy and innovation education: Setting a new paradigm in graphic design education. *Design Learning for Tomorrow*, 2.

Appiah, E., & Cronjé, J. (2014). The influence of information and communication technology on graphic design: Reflections on pedagogy. *Journal of Science and Technology (Ghana)*, *34*(1), 85–94.

Abrahams, M. (2014). *Making sense of the transitional maelstroms of part-time students and their conceptions of learning as mediated by contextual domains of work, family and self*. Paper developed as part of the SAQA-University of the Western Cape Research Partnership for the research Lifelong Learning and National Qualifications Frameworks.

Blair, B. (2006). At the end of a huge crit in the summer, it was "crap": I'd worked really hard but all she said was "fine" and I was gutted. *Art, Design & Communication in Higher Education*, *5*(2).

Chafeker, A. (2016, June 9). *Open and Alternative Architectural Education: The Case of Open Architecture*. In-venue and online CPD event for the Cape Institute for Architecture (CIfA). Retrieved from http://openarchitecture.co.za/video-cifa-cpd-02

De La Harpe, B., Peterson, J. F., Frankham, N., Zehner, R., Neale, D., Musgrave, E., & McDermott, R. (2009). Assessment focus in studio: What is most prominent in architecture, art and design? *International Journal of Art & Design Education*, *28*(1), 37–51.

Ellmers, G., & Foley, M. (2007). Introducing reflective strategies informed by problem-based learning to enhance cognitive participation and knowledge transference in graphic design education. In *Proceedings of connected international conference on design education*. Sydney: University of New South Wales.

Hammersley, A., Tallantyre, F., & Le Cornu, A. (2013). Flexible learning: A practical guide for academic staff. *Higher Education Academy*, York.

Ivala, E., & Gachago, D. (2012). Social media for enhancing student engagement: The use of Facebook and blogs at a university of technology. *South African Journal of Higher Education, 26*(1), 152–167.

Johnston, S. (1997). Introducing and supporting change towards more flexible teaching approaches. In *Proceedings of the Cambridge international conference on open and distance learning: The convergence of distance and conventional education: Patterns of flexibility for the individual learner.* Cambridge: Open University. ISBN 0-7492-8849-3.

Jones, B., & Walters, S. (2015). Flexible learning and teaching: Looking beyond the binary of full-time/part-time provision in South African higher education. *Critical Studies in Teaching and Learning, 3*(1), 61–84.

Kettle, J. (2013). Flexible pedagogies: Employer engagement and work-based learning. *Higher Education.* Retrieved from www.heacademy.ac.uk/system/files/resources/ee_wbl_report.pdf

Kuhn, S. (2001). Learning from the architecture studio: Implications for project-based pedagogy. *International Journal of Engineering Education, 17*(4/5), 349–352.

Lymer, G. (2009). Demonstrating professional vision: The work of critique in architectural education. *Mind, Culture, and Activity, 16*(2), 145–171.

Maher, M. L., & Simoff, S. J. (2000). Collaboratively designing within the design. In *Collaborative design* (pp. 391–399). London: Springer.

Morkel, J. (2013). Designing authentic architectural education for the future: A case for Open Architecture. *Architecture South Africa: Journal of the South African Institute of Architects, 64*, 19–20.

Morkel, J. (2016a, March 17–18). *You have to break it to make it: Reflecting on the open architecture pilot.* Presentation at the ICT in Higher Education Conference, Sandton, Johannesburg. Unpublished presentation.

Morkel, J. (2016b). *First stir and then blend it: Lessons learnt from a pilot programme in architecture.* Seminar presented for e/merge Africa at The University of Cape Town. Retrieved from http://emergeafrica.net/first-stir-and-then-blend-it/

Morkel, J. (2016c, May 17). *Blended and beyond.* CPUT Teaching and Learning with Technology Day, SARATEC, Bellville, South Africa. Unpublished presentation.

Morkel, J. (2017, May 15–19). *Listen, look, learn and take the leap: Developing a blended architecture studio.* Big Ideas Speaker at the international online LX Conference. Unpublished presentation.

Outram, S. (2009). Flexible Learning Pathfinders: A review of the pilots final and interim reports'. *The Higher Education Academy.* Retrieved from www.heacademy. ac.uk/resources/detail/Flexible_learning_pathfinders_a_review

Pearce, C. (2017). *Experiential Program for Continued Professional Development Department of Architectural Technology & Interior Design in conjunction with Open Architecture Workbook for Step-Up: Build Effective Practice Workshop.* Unpublished manuscript.

Poulsen, L., & Morkel, J. (2016). Open architecture: A blended learning model for architectural education. *Architecture South Africa: Journal of the South African Institute of Architects, 78*, 28–30.

Ryan, A., & Tilbury, D. (2013). Flexible pedagogies: Preparing for the future. *Higher Education Academy*. Retrieved from http://flexed.sfu.ca/wpcontent/uploads/2014/10/npi_report.pdf

Shulman, L. S. (2005). Signature pedagogies in the professions. *Daedalus, 134*(3), 52–59.

Van Graan, A. (2014). *Open Architecture: SAIA's Success Story*. Retrieved from www.youtube.com/watch?v=SZAezvvj5g4&t=7s

Van Graan, A. (2016, June 9). *Open and Alternative Architectural Education: The case of OpenArchitecture*. In-venue and online CPD event for the Cape Institute for Architecture (CIfA). Retrieved from http://openarchitecture.co.za/video-cifa-cpd-02

Walters, S., Witbooi, S., & Abrahams, M. (2015). Keeping the doors of learning open for adult student-workers within higher education. *The Adult Learner, Irish Journal of Adult and Community Education*. Retrieved from https://www.aontas.com/assets/resources/Adult-Learner-Journal/AONTAS%20Adult%20Learner%20Journal%202015.pdf

Webster, H. (2005). The architectural review: A study of ritual, acculturation and reproduction in architectural education. *Arts and Humanities in Higher Education, 4*(3), 265–282.

Zimmerman, B. J. (2008). Investigating self-regulation and motivation: Historical background, methodological developments, and future prospects. *American Educational Research Journal, 45*(1), 166–183.

Theme 2

What strategies are utilized or could be utilized at Cape Peninsula University of Technology in Cape Town, South Africa, to guarantee fair access to qualified individuals in management, staffing and student recruitment from all cultural backgrounds?

3 Student Engagement Strategies in Higher Education

Change, Transition and Student Leadership

Xena Cupido and Najwa Norodien-Fataar

Introduction

The Need for a Transformed Higher Education

Higher education institutions (HEIs) in South Africa (SA) have recently experienced significant shifts, as the collective student body called for a radical transformation in academic discourse and practice. The call for change could be witnessed in the 2015 and 2016 student protests that challenged the academic status quo at various HEIs across SA, resulting in discussions and debates and, in some cases, division with regard to the call for decolonized and free education. The uprising revealed that although there have been significant shifts in what was once considered "a fragmented and structurally racialised system . . . to a relatively more integrated system" (Blom, 2015, p. 5), transformation has remained elusive (Department of Higher Education and Training, 2016). The student protests exposed HEIs as constituting a fractured system not wholly transformed as envisioned. Yet, evidence of this fragmentation was succinctly documented in the Soudien Report (Soudien, 2008), as it is commonly referred to, describing institutional cultures at HEIs in a post-apartheid SA as alienating and disempowering, reminiscent of a value system which once promoted inequalities (Department of Higher Education and Training, 2016).

An interesting observation contained in the report revealed that despite the existence of institutional policies addressing transformation, practices were not aligned with the lived experience of staff and students in relation to teaching and learning, curriculum development, language, residence life and governance. This could possibly be attributed to "poor dissemination of information pertaining to policy, limited awareness of policies, a lack of awareness of the roles and responsibilities pertaining to implementation that flow from the policies, and a lack of institutional will" (Department of Education, 2008, p. 14). However, it begs the question of whether HEIs are serious enough about transformation as the lack of stakeholder engagement continues to be a challenge in setting the transformation agenda as outlined by the Department of Education (2008). It is clear that South African higher education policy is explicitly committed to widening participation through equitable access to groups previously underrepresented. Evidence of this can be found in the National Plan for Higher Education in South Africa (Ministry of Education, 2001, p. 6), where the following objective was outlined to develop a system of higher education that will "promote equity of access and fair chances of success to all who are seeking to realise their potential through higher education, while eradicating all forms of unfair discrimination and advancing redress for past inequalities".

Since then, universities have faced increasing student enrolment numbers from varying demographic, cultural, intellectual and linguistic backgrounds, challenging the hegemony of HEIs (Department of Education, 2008). Boughey (2007) recognized, in the face of this reality, the need for institutional development that would focus on "systemic and institutional efficiency to support the teaching and learning process" (p. 3). Similarly, Devlin (2013) suggested a shift in institutional practices to create an engaging supportive learning environment for students. Researchers such as Du Preez, Steenkamp and Baard (2013) and Wilson-Strydom (2011) have argued that a social justice approach is essential, one that recognizes the educationally disadvantaged, marginalized and excluded. More important, an approach is needed that creates an environment that enables access, with substantial academic and social support. This becomes possible when the diverse needs of students are factored into support programmes (Trotter & Roberts, 2006). How to ensure this type of student support and participation remains a fundamental higher education concern? Surveys such as the South African Survey of Student Engagement, as noted by Strydom & Mentz (2010), strongly argued that HEIs needed to engage with students to understand the student experience and thereby improve student success.

The aim of this chapter is to focus on a peer tutor programme at one university of technology as a means to enhance student success and engagement. The peer tutor programme is part of the institutional support structure of the university, designed to support students and lecturers in their teaching and learning activities. Success is defined here as premised on the meaning suggested by Kuh (2008):

[N]ot only whether students have earned a degree, but also whether graduates are in fact achieving the level of preparation—in terms of knowledge, capabilities, and personal qualities—that will enable them to both thrive and contribute in a fast-changing economy and in turbulent, highly demanding global, societal and often personal contexts.

(p. 2)

Against this background, and the recent student call to address transformation at South African HEIs, we reflect on the student experience of their engagement in a peer-support programme. This chapter considers how institutional support programmes such as a peer tutor programme enhance students' educational engagement by exploring their experiences of engaging in such a programme.

A Peer Tutor Support Programme

The peer tutor programme, which is the focus of this research, is regarded as a key institutional teaching and learning support mechanism designed to enhance student engagement, retention and success at the universities of technology. The peer tutor system has been recognized as one of the ways in which access to knowledge and skills at the university is provided so that students are able to fully participate in sense-making and knowledge-generating activities (Layton & McKenna, 2016). Considered an integral component in higher education, peer-support programmes are encouraged and widely implemented. We suggest that peer tutoring is a crucial mechanism for the advancement of student engagement and learning. Other than student engagement, Layton and McKenna (2016) recognized the relational value of the peer tutor system as one in which peer tutors could develop partnerships with academic staff and through personal interaction with other students. They suggest that the role-modelling aspects within the tutorial programme can be considered an enabling factor, which encourages students to persist through the modelling of academic skills.

   Peer tutoring has shown that it has a role to play in supporting students in higher education with regard to the transition from school to university as well as from university to the world of work (Lizzio, 2006). It is widely recognized as an effective tool in retaining students through the support that it not only provides but also seeks to foster a sense of belonging with the university community. Aside from the academic endeavour, as an inclusionary mechanism, tutorial programmes have the potential to effect real transformational changes by developing a student's sense of connection, capability, resourcefulness and purpose, which, in turn, help to develop academic identity (Lizzio, 2006). Researchers such as Kift (2009) and Lizzio (2006) have shown that peer tutor programmes provide a student engagement strategy that has the potential to retain and support students. Academic support programmes such as peer tutoring assist in engaging students and in facilitating connections between staff and other students in which dialogue and feedback can take place (Leach & Zepke, 2011).

Conceptual Framework

This chapter utilizes the Solomonides multidimensional model of student engagement in combination with Lizzio's (2006) Five Senses Framework to understand students' experiences of their engagement in a peer tutor programme, an essential institutional teaching and learning support mechanism in HEIs. We suggest that both models allow us to explore the affective dimensions of students' engagement in higher education. These models indicate that students' feelings of connectedness and belonging are central to successful engagement at the university. Solomonides' (2013) and Lizzio's (2006) conceptual frameworks both emphasize the affective factors of students' engagement, such as students' sense of self, belonging and alienation, as crucial in discussing transformation in HEIs.

In South Africa, we have used the American National Survey of Student Engagement (NSSE) known as the South African Survey of Student Engagement (SASSE) to understand student engagement. Solomonides (2013) cautions that norms associated with engagement surveys are conceptualized against predetermined pedagogic practices rather than against students' experiences. He suggested the need for a multidimensional approach to understanding the complexities of the student experience of engagement and that represents a holistic view of student engagement. Student engagement measures have to be sensitive to the ways in which students live out the intersections among life, learning and work across different contexts. Solomonides (2013) identified students' sense of being and sense of transformation as central to the multidimensional model of student engagement. Students' sense of being is regarded as the "affective relationships within students' learning and the innate ways in which students might be relating to their formal and informal learning" (Solomonides, 2013, p. 52). At the same time, students' sense of transformation is seen as "not only integrating knowledge and experience but also the process of integrating the various outcomes of learning with the students' sense of being" (Solomonides, 2013, p. 52). He identified students' sense of being professional, students' sense of discipline knowledge and students' sense of engagement as essential elements of the multidimensional model which are in "a dynamic relationship" with students' sense of being and sense of transformation. Unlike Leach and Zepke (2011), who regard students' relationship with their studies as transactional, Solomonides (2013) argued that the ontological dimensions of student engagement in HEIs are fundamental to ensure successful student engagement.

Lizzio's (2006) Five Senses Framework provided valuable indicators to consider for student success. This theory highlights the factors that are more likely to lead to student satisfaction, engagement and retention in higher education. The framework identifies five areas on which transition strategies could be positioned without being prescriptive about solutions: capability, connectedness, purpose, resourcefulness and culture (Lizzio, 2006). For the purpose of this chapter, we focused on the sense of connection students develop through their engagement with a peer tutor programme. In this framework, a sense of connection is seen as building relationships with other students, staff and the university, which is of critical importance for student engagement, transition and leadership development. Students with stronger connections are more likely to be successful learners, effective colleagues and happy people.

Lizzio's framework describes the various stages of transition, such as student identity development from entry into university to the development of a graduate identity on exiting the system. It is important to recognize that transition issues are different for incoming and final-year students; however, it is our contention that the transitioning needs of students at these various stages provide opportunities for engagement between the institution and the student and that some of these could in part be addressed through a peer tutoring programme.

The framework provided us with further conceptual lenses to explore students' experiences of the peer tutor programme. Lizzio's (2006) student life-cycle model provided indicators and possible areas of development that emphasized the affective dimensions of student engagement. He suggested that the affective factors of student engagement address issues of inclusion and contribute to productive student engagement. Rather than an exclusive focus on knowledge acquisition as a successful form of engagement, students' ontological engagement is highlighted as equally significant for successful student engagement and transformation in higher education.

Research Design

The aim of this research, which data is presented in this chapter was to investigate students' experience of peer tutoring at a university. A mixed-methods research approach with a sequential design (Creswell, Plano, Clark, Gutmann, & Hanson, 2003) was used in order to gain an in-depth perspective into students' experiences of the peer tutor programme. The research was guided by the following overall research questions:

1. How has the peer tutor programme influenced students' experiences of engagement at a university of technology?
2. How has participating in the peer tutor programme contributed to academic leadership?

Quantitative data was collected using an online self-administered questionnaire, adapted from Lizzio's (2006) Five Senses Model. The online questionnaire focused on students' perceptions of the tutor programmes, the perceived benefits, the unexpected benefits and the knowledge and skills developed and/or enhanced through the programme. Students were also asked to make recommendations to improve the programme and what was required to enhance their engagement experience. The results of the quantitative data were analysed descriptively. The data from the quantitative findings assisted in developing the questions for the focus-group discussions. The data from the focus-group discussions were analysed through a coding process and triangulated with the quantitative data.

The project was divided into two phases. The first phase consisted of an extensive 97-item questionnaire based on Lizzio's (2006) Five Senses Framework.[1] The questionnaire was adapted and sent via email to all students who were registered and trained as tutors by the student learning unit in which the tutor training programme was located.

All students in the database from 2013 were included in the call. The reason for the retrospective approach was to ensure that a sufficient number of students were included. Approximately 350 students were emailed the link to the online self-administered questionnaire. A total of 61 students completed the online questionnaire, resulting in a response rate of 17.4%. At the end of the questionnaire, students were asked if they were willing to participate in a focus-group discussion in Phase 2 of the project. Students who were interested were requested to include their contact details. In Phase 2, the students who indicated their willingness to participate in a focus-group discussion were invited to attend. The focus-group discussions were guided by a set of broad questions, emanating from the data of the survey questionnaire. The focus-group discussions were recorded, with the permission of the participants, and transcribed and coded.

The project received research funding from the Research and Innovation Fund for Teaching and Learning (RIFTAL)[2] and received ethical clearance from the university. Full informed consent was obtained from participants prior to the study and permission was granted for the data to be used in scholarly work and research publications. Throughout the research process, confidentiality was maintained.

Description of the Sample

All faculties at the university were represented in the first phase of the research project, with the Faculty of Business and Management Sciences having the largest representation of 21 (34%) students. Applied Sciences 13 (21%), followed by 11 (18%) of students from Informatics and Design; Health and Wellness Sciences, Engineering and Education had lower representation.

The low engineering representation could be attributed to the fact that the Engineering Faculty manages its own tutor training which is decentralized from the student learning unit. In terms of the level of study the participants were in, the largest (31%) of students were registered in their second year, followed by third-year students at 26%, fourth-year (BTech) students at 25% and master's students at 2.4%.

Two focus-group discussions were scheduled and 27 (44%) participants indicated their interest in attending. Eventually, 21 students attended, a response rate of 78%.

Students were asked if they had been tutored previously and the majority (72.9%) indicated that they had been tutored before, and 98.2% had successfully completed the tutor training programme. The two themes that emerged from the focus-group discussions and online questionnaire are discussed in the following.

Developing a Sense of Connection With Other Students

In the effort to understand students' experiences of their engagement on the peer tutoring programme, this section focuses on how students build connections with other students at the university through the peer tutoring programme. By means of Lizzio's (2006) Five Senses Framework, students were asked to reflect on the connections made with other students and with the university through their participation in the tutorial programme. Case (2007) suggested that "engagement can be considered to represent a connection in the context of a relationship which a student desires or expects to belong to" (p. 120). The findings showed that students, through their interactions with other students, developed a personal sense of connection with fellow students (70.2%). This was also reflected in their responses in the focus-group discussions as they indicated that while the peer tutor programme focused on academic engagement, they developed a better understanding of students from different cultural backgrounds other than their own. The process of engaging with students of diverse backgrounds developed an appreciation of difference in interactions between students. Students expressed a sense of empathy towards other students as they talked about the struggles that incoming students experienced: One student commented,

> I decided to become a tutor because in my department many students were failing . . . to assist them with some explanations. Also to be close with [*sic*] them and if they need my assistance, they can easily contact me.

This quotation suggests that students were interested in developing greater connections with other students at the university. The tutors were aware that students were not doing well and that they required more than just academic support: they wanted to be "close to them" to provide more emotional support. Statements such as these denote the personal connection that students developed with one another through the peer tutor programme.

Students indicated that they were given the opportunity to work with senior tutors in the programme and that helped them to learn from and model their own behaviour on successful students. This included motivating students to persevere, showing interest in the course and the student tutee, and simply dedicating their own time and energy. During the focus-group discussions, one student explained the crucial role of the tutor programme in forming connections with other students:

> When I came here, I did not know many students, I knew the faces. But . . .
> the tutoring programme connected me to other students.

Students thus valued the relationships with other students on the peer tutor programme. The statement by the student is corroborated by Layton and McKenna (2016), who argued that relationships are central to the tutorial offering. Besides the benefits of small-group learning, and engaging with other students, peer-to-peer engagement contributed to an increase in students' sense of belonging and self. Wimpenny and Savin-Baden (2013) suggested that connecting with peers decreased the sense of disconnection that students could experience at university. The university experience is therefore less isolating or alienating, as students develop personal connections with others (Cartney & Rouse, 2006, p. 88).

Besides building connections with other students, our data showed that affective factors such as confidence, respect, willingness to help other students and developing friendships were key concerns for students engaging on the peer tutor programme. Case (2007) suggested the affective dimensions of learning, such as students' passion and inspiration, were important considerations when exploring student engagement in HEIs. A student commented, "I have the confidence to speak to a large group of individuals without feeling nervous". Another student explained that he had "learnt to interact with others". The students' also emphasized self-improvement: "I learnt about the abilities I possess, and self-growth and developing a sense of self". One student commented that she thought peer tutoring was a life-affirming experience. She commented that "the tutoring was one of the most beautiful experiences of my life, something I will take [with me] in [my] life experiences [*sic*]; tutoring is not only for university but for everyday life". These comments show that students' sense of being and sense of self were important to their engagement with their studies and that they gained valuable affective skills through their engagement with the peer tutor programme.

Another significant finding was the development of leadership skills through the programme, denoting employment prospects. This was captured in a student's statement:

> By being a tutor, I have learnt the different methods of learning from other students. Also, I can talk to everyone in my class. Tutoring is the environment whereby you tell students how to approach a situation in terms of solving a question.

This statement suggests that peer tutors had to develop a set of skills useful in the academic environment as well as in the world of work. Through the peer tutor programme, they develop attributes needed to be able to solve problems, identify the needs of others, and devise appropriate solutions to challenging situations. Having a deeper understanding of their own subject knowledge is referred to by Solomonides (2013) as developing a sense of discipline knowledge. Similarly, Lizzio (2006) refers to this as their developing a sense of purpose and a sense of their vocation. This sense of discipline knowledge is helpful as students are confronted with various academic challenges and are able to plan and prepare through the identification of relevant and purposeful activities to engage students during tutorial sessions. Keenan (2014) argued that being confronted with challenges such as these develop flexibility and adaptability, resulting in an enhanced ability for problem solving.

Institutional Support for the Peer Tutoring Programme

In this section, we discuss the participants' experiences of the kinds of institutional support they received as tutors on the peer tutoring programme. Zepke and Leach (2010) suggested institutional support is key to providing students with an environment conducive to learning. Lizzio (2006) proposed the need for students to develop a sense of resourcefulness and that universities can assist students to be more resourceful through the provision of clear and accessible roles, procedures and resources and encouraging timely help-seeking behaviour. Results showed that students were not adequately supported by the university infrastructure.

The students felt that besides monetary reimbursement, they needed to be rewarded for the service they offered to the university. Students noted that incentives such as printing bytes, stationery and equipment were not available to support their tutoring and suggested these could be offered to them as incentives.

Another key factor that students were concerned about was the way in which the administrative issues were dealt with by the university. They explained that the "tutor supervisors need to carry out "their end of the deal," i.e. transportation of documents (claim forms) to the respective office(s); regular check-ups to ensure that the tutoring programme is being carried out effectively". Students complained that forms were lost or misplaced multiple times and that they often were not paid. The results further showed tutors' perceived lack of educational support from the lecturers:

> Every three months in the programme the lecturers need to check on the tutors and I think it will be much better if the lecturers can attend one of the tutor classes to check if we cover the content and the rest of each chapter effectively. They need to follow the tutors closely by telling them what they are doing wrong.

Participants indicated that they needed more mentoring in the tutorial programme from their lecturers. Some students revealed that lecturers did not timetable tutorials and venues, and expected students to find these on their own. It is evident from the above accounts that tutors need greater recognition and increased support from lecturers and heads of department in faculties.

A striking feature emerging from the data is the tutors' lack of knowledge of the ethos of the university. Students felt that while the tutoring programme enabled them to engage with the department in which they were registered, they did not feel connected to the university and struggled to understand the values of the institution. "I really do not know the values; I am not sure about the values but I know about 'innovation and excellence'". This statement indicates that while the students participated actively in their learning through the peer tutoring programme, the university did not invest in providing adequate support for the tutors.

The findings showed that the student tutors struggled for recognition at the university. Their frustration at navigating the formal structures of the university, such as administrative structures, to ensure timely payment, find venues for tutorials, obtain resources for tutorial classes and obtain mentoring support from lecturers, prevented them from developing the "sense of resourcefulness" and hampered their "sense of engagement" at the university (Lizzio, 2006, Solomonides, 2013). While the university provided a peer tutor programme for students, the processes, procedures and resources available to students were inadequate and hampered student and institutional relationships and, therefore, tutors' sense of connection to the institution.

Conclusion

This chapter reflected on the student experience of peer tutoring at a university of technology in the context of the increased university enrolments of students from diverse demographic, cultural, intellectual and linguistic backgrounds.

The demand for a transformed higher education and continuing student protests signalled the urgent need for HEIs to address their institutional cultures and recognize the needs of previously under representative groups.

This chapter showed that while there are many factors that impact student engagement, transition and the development of leadership skills, the peer tutor programme played a significant role in developing students' affective engagement, such as a sense of connection and a sense of belonging to their peers and to their studies. Peer-to-peer engagement was crucial in cultivating a sense of connection to their studies. A key finding of this study was the importance of a peer tutor programme as a student engagement strategy, beyond the academic support provided. The affective relationships that developed among students created a sense of connectedness and belonging and, in turn, enhanced their engagement experience. Through engagement in the tutorial programme, students developed a sense of self and leadership, thereby creating new opportunities for personal growth.

On the other hand, findings showed that while peer engagement was enabling to students, their sense of connection to the institution was constrained by inadequate policies, processes and procedures to support the peer-support programmes. Thus, while student tutors formed firm connections with other students, they felt marginalized by the university processes and as they encountered poor administration of the tutorial programme, inadequate incentives and the absence of mentorship from lecturers. These factors made them feel less connected to the values and the ethos of the university. We believe that these factors are important in order to build a transformed university.

We recommend that HEIs do more to support tutors through making the necessary resources available to enhance student engagement. Extending resources to the peer tutor programme creates greater opportunities for creating a sense of connection to the university.

We conclude that the peer tutor programme offers students and HEIs more than just an academic opportunity but, rather, an opportunity to address students' transformational issues and their lack of connection with the institution. Inadequate and outdated practices and policies need to be addressed to counter students' sense of alienation. Even though support programmes such as the peer tutor programme play a significant role in peer engagement and peer learning, the institutional systems supporting these programmes are unsatisfactory. While the focus on transformation in HEIs addresses the curriculum, language policies and teaching and learning approaches, this chapter shows that institutional support structures and programmes are pivotal to addressing the needs of our students and the institutional cultures of HEIs. Other institutional support structures in which such programmes are located require further exploration. We recommend that further studies investigate how such systems impact transformation in HEI.

Notes

1. Permission was granted by Prof. Lizzio to use the Five Senses Framework.
2. RIFTAL is a university research grant.

References

Blom, R. (2015). Cited by Keet, A. Second Higher Education Summit, 15–17 October 2015. Annexure 10. Institutional Cultures/Environments. Briefing paper prepared for the second national Higher Education Transformation Summit, 2015. Department of Higher Education and Training. South Africa.

Boughey, C. (2007). Educational development in South Africa: From social reproduction to capitalist expansion? *Higher Education Policy, 20*(1), 5–18.

Cartney, P., & Rouse, A. (2006). The emotional impact of learning in small groups: Highlighting the impact on student progression and retention. *Teaching in Higher Education, 11*(1), 79–91.

Case, J. (2007). Alienation and engagement: Exploring students' experiences of studying engineering. *Teaching in Higher Education, 12*(1), 119–133.

Creswell, J. W., Plano Clark, V. L., Gutmann, M., & Hanson, W. (2003). Advanced mixed methods research designs. In A. Tashakkori & C. Teddlie (Eds.), *Handbook on mixed methods in the behavioral and social sciences* (pp. 209–240). Thousand Oaks, CA: Sage Publications.

Department of Education. (2008). *Report of the ministerial committee on transformation and social cohesion and the elimination of discrimination in public higher education institutions*. Pretoria: Department of Education.

Department of Higher Education and Training. (2016). *Report on the second national higher education transformation summit, Durban, KwaZulu-Natal, 15–17 October 2015*. Pretoria: Department of Higher Education and Training.

Devlin, M. (2013). Bridging socio-cultural incongruity: Conceptualising the success of students from low socio-economic status backgrounds in Australian higher education. *Studies in Higher Education, 38*(6), 939–949.

Du Preez, R., Steenkamp, L. P., & Baard, R. S. (2013). An investigation into a peer module mentoring programme in economic and management sciences. *International Business & Economics Research Journal, 12*(10), 1225–1237.

Keenan, C. (2014). *Mapping student-led peer learning in the UK*. York: The Higher Education Academy.

Kift, S. (2009). *Articulating a transition pedagogy to scaffold and to enhance the first year student learning experience in Australian higher education: Final report for ALTC senior fellowship program*. Strawberry Hills, NSW: Australian Learning and Teaching Council.

Kuh, G. D. (2008). Excerpt from *High-impact educational practices: What they are, who has access to them, and why they matter*. Washington, DC: Association of American Colleges and Universities.

Layton, D., & McKenna, S. (2016). Partnerships and parents: Relationships in tutorial programmes. *Higher Education Research & Development, 35*(2), 296–308.

Student Engagement Strategies in HE 49

Leach, L., & Zepke, N. (2011). Engaging students in learning: A review of a conceptual organiser. *Higher Education Research & Development*, *30*(2), 193–204.

Lizzio, A. (2006). *Designing an orientation and transition strategy for commencing students: A conceptual summary of research and practice: Griffith first year experience project*. Brisbane: Griffith University.

Ministry of Education. (2001). Draft National Plan for Higher Education in South Africa. Retrieved from http://www.dhet.gov.za/HED%20Policies/National%20Plan%20on%20Higher%20Education.pdf

Solomonides, I. (2013). A relational and multi-dimensional model of student engagement. In E. Dunne & D. Owen (Eds.), *The student engagement handbook: Practice in higher education* (pp. 43–58). Bingley: Emerald.

Soudien, C. (2008). The intersection of race and class in the South African university: Student experiences. *South African Journal of Higher Education*, *22*(3), 662–678.

Strydom, J. F., & Mentz, M. (2010). *Focusing the student experience on success through student engagement*. Pretoria: Council on Higher Education.

Trotter, E., & Roberts, C. A. (2006). Enhancing the early student experience. *Higher Education Research & Development*, *25*(4), 371–386.

Wilson-Strydom, M. (2011). University access for social justice: A capabilities perspective. *South African Journal of Education*, *31*(3), 407–418.

Wimpenny, K., & Savin-Baden, M. (2013). Alienation, agency and authenticity: A synthesis of the literature on student engagement. *Teaching in Higher Education*, *18*(3), 311–326.

Zepke, N., & Leach, L. (2010). Improving student engagement: Ten proposals for action. *Active Learning in Higher Education*, *11*(3), 167–177.

Theme 3

What approaches are being utilized or could be utilized at Cape Peninsula University of Technology in Cape Town, South Africa, to create and advance diverse and multicultural teaching practices and programming?

4 Looking Beyond Inequalities

Embracing Transformation in the South African Higher Education System

Zilungile Sosibo

Introduction

Globally, education is hailed as the most important driver of social and economic growth and development of a country, and also as the most powerful instrument for reducing poverty and inequality (Patrinos, 2016). Wanjohi (2011) asserts that education brings about socio-economic empowerment and prosperity, and intellectual transformation and self-development. Therefore, the contribution of education to development cannot be overstated.

It is a widely held view that education is a basic and fundamental human right. Yet in South Africa (SA), where inequalities abound and transformation is slow, education appears to be a right to a selected few (Maimela, 2015, p. 5). This is despite the fact that access to higher education (HE) now includes those groups that were previously marginalized during the apartheid system. The SA education system is fraught with transformation-related challenges. This situation highlights the need for the government/state and higher education institutions (HEIs) to formulate policies, practices and initiatives that would advance the transformation of HEIs in post-apartheid SA.

This chapter presents a synopsis of the most pressing transformational challenges that have and still continue to plague the South African HE system. Granted, this system is faced with ginormous transformational challenges that are beyond the scope of this chapter. The focus of this paper is on poor student performance and diminishing financial support for HE. These challenges are then juxtaposed with the policies, practices and initiatives introduced by the government through the Department of Higher Education and Training (DHET) and by HEIs in an effort to embrace transformation of the South African HE system. In this chapter, it is argued that enormous as the transformation-related challenges are, government and universities are not oblivious to the plight of students affected by them. Rather, they make efforts to minimize challenges and to make universities places of effective teaching and learning for all.

Synopsis of the South African HE System

After 1994, the Government of South Africa, through *The White Paper 3: A Programme for the Transformation of HE* (Department of Education, 1997) sought to make education accessible to all the students regardless of race, socio-economic class, gender or nationality. This was an effort to redress gross inequalities that were created by the apartheid system. Prior to 1994, Black students were confined in historically Black universities (HBUs). With the advent of democracy in 1994 and the release of the 1997 *White Paper 3*, historically White universities (HWUs) became accessible to all the students regardless of their backgrounds. Consequently, Black students began to flock to HWUs, a process known as massification of education (Kraak, 2000). This trend still continues. However, there are concerns that equality of opportunity for all students has not yet been realized. Disparities in the success rate of students from different socio-economic and racial backgrounds still exist. Malele (2011) argues that poor student success rate in the public HEIs illustrates the dysfunctionality of this education system. In addition, funding for HE is still fraught with challenges, which reflects the failure by HEIs to embrace diversity, inclusiveness and transformation.

Poor Student Performance

The South African HE system is known for its low student participation, outputs and throughputs and high attrition and failure rates (du Preez, Simmonds, & Verhoef, 2016). Even though access to HE for students from historically disadvantaged socio-economic backgrounds has increased dramatically, access rates have not translated to high success rates (CHE, 2013a). Instead, low success rates for these students continue unabated. High access, coupled with high failure and attrition rates and disproportionately low output and throughput rates in South African HEIs at both undergraduate and postgraduate levels, has been widely documented (CHE, 2013a, 2013b).

According to the CHE (2015, p. 3), "[a] substantial improvement in equity of opportunity and outcomes for students remains an elusive transformational goal." This statement points to the fact that universities are failing the transformation agenda. The CHE further highlights the high rates of students who fail to graduate within regulation time. Delays in student graduation are costly to the state and taxpayers who fund HE. To emphasize this point, CHE (2015) provides statistics from CHE's VitalStats 2013, which illustrate that only 27% of the 2006 cohorts, 20% of the 2007 cohorts and 29% of the 2008 cohorts completed their diploma and degree studies within the stipulated time, and only 5% of Black and Coloured youth succeed in HE (CHE, 2013b). These delays are inevitable in a system that is faced with myriad challenges related to poor funding mechanisms, poor student support, racial discrimination and colonized curriculum. I agree with Wilson-Strydom (2015, p. 2) who contends that "[w]here universities increase access without improving chances of success, they create new forms of injustice whilst seeking to overcome old forms." Therefore, there is a need for the South African HE to match access with success.

Another factor that compromises the performance of university students in SA is poor academic support for especially those from racially, socio-economically and linguistically disadvantaged backgrounds. The need for support for students from these backgrounds has been documented in existing literature (Sosibo & Katiya, 2015). Two theories justify this need. One is articulation gap between school and university knowledge (Wilson-Strydom, 2015), which simply means that when some students enter university, they come with inferior knowledge that is not compatible with the knowledge taught at university. Conley (2008) argues that being eligible for university does not equate to being prepared/ready for university.

Evidently, this deficit model puts the blame on students and portrays them as inadequate and ill prepared for university. It seems to assume that universities need to develop the capabilities of students for university readiness and smooth transitioning. Wilson-Strydom (2015) proposes a list of capabilities that should be developed in students to prepare them for university entrance. For further reading, see Wilson-Strydom (2015, p. 4).

The second theory which stands in juxtapose to the preceding one casts doubt on the readiness of universities to create friendly, supportive and enabling spaces for students from previously disadvantaged groups to succeed. This theory portrays universities as creating an environment that is difficult for some students to penetrate. Schreiner and Hulme (2009) suggest that when designing and implementing educational programmes, universities should take cognizance of the diverse needs of students from different backgrounds. University curriculum is also seen by some students and academics as rigid and colonized. The 2015 student movements, #RhodesMustFall and #FeesMustFall erupted at the University of Cape Town (UCT) in Cape Town and Wits University in Johannesburg. The statue of the colonialist, Cecil John Rhodes, which stood at the centre of UCT, led to the #RhodesMustFall movement (Universities South Africa, 2015). Students used this campaign to force the removal of this statue from the university grounds, on the basis that they felt that it was the epitome, symbol and constant reminder of the apartheid system that permeated UCT, thus affecting this institution's culture.

The removal of the Rhodes statue symbolized victory for students against the oppressive racial system that they felt characterized UCT and other HWIs. The #FeesMustFall movement was a reaction to the reduction of university subsidy by the state, which created a void that led to serious challenges for students from low socio-economic backgrounds to afford university tuition. Suffice to say that these movements succeeded in highlighting the plight of students from previously disadvantaged backgrounds and the inherent challenges in the HE system. Not only this, but they also sparked action and debates towards the discourse of decolonizing curriculum and widespread inequalities and racism in the HE system.

Racial discrimination has been found to be another factor that adversely affects the performance of some students. This type of discrimination is pervasive in South African universities and mostly in the HWUs (The MOCR on Transformation in South African Public Universities, 2013). During the 2nd National HE Summit in 2015, the then minister of HE and training, Dr Blade Nzimande, expressed deep concern about the continued presence of racism and discrimination in universities. This was after the wake of student movements, such as the Open Stellenbosch Movement and the transformation battles at North West University and #RhodesMustFall alluded to earlier. At this summit, Nzimande encouraged universities to ensure that they improved institutional cultures for all students and that they became places of tolerance where all students felt welcome.

Alongside racial discrimination is what students describe as colonized education. This factor revolves around the politics of epistemology which raises questions about whose knowledge is worth and how universities teach epistemic knowledge that is relevant to students' contexts and identities. Fataar (2017, p. 1) avers that colonization means that "the knowledge systems of colonized groups, non-Europeans, indigenous folk, etc. were suppressed . . . leading to the failure to incorporate such knowledge into formal functioning of society and its school and university curricula." Students feel that university curriculum is decontextualized from their own realities and that it dehumanises them (Jansen, in van Heerden, 2017). Nonetheless, Jansen questions this thought, claiming that it was racist professors (not curriculum) that dehumanised him as a student. Granted, Jansen's debate is centred on the semantics and not so much on the politics of colonialism. In his speech at the 2015 Summit, Nzimande called for the decolonisation of university curriculum and the Africanisation of universities. Le Grange (2016) highlights the importance of decolonising South African university curriculum but mentions that decolonisation is a process that takes time and not an event.

Staffing is increasingly becoming a serious problem in the South African HE system (Bozzoli, 2015). The DHET (2013, p. 35) indicates that increase in students' enrolments over the past 20 years "has not been accompanied by an equivalent expansion in the number of academics," resulting in heavy teaching workloads for lecturers due to disproportionate student: lecturer ratios. Adding to this challenge is the ageing professoriate, low levels of staff academic qualifications and low levels of high-skills production (The MOCR on Transformation in South African Public Universities, 2013). The Academy of Science of South Africa (ASSAF) (2010) reveals that only 34% of university staff holds PhDs. This percentage provides a gloomy picture if set against the National Development Plan (NDP), which sets a target of 75% of academic staff with PhDs in 2030 (National Planning Commission, 2012). This situation impacts not only the provision of high-quality teaching and learning to students but research outputs as well.

There is also a perception that university staff remains predominantly White and male, with little effort to grow Black male and female academics (The MOCR on Transformation in South African Public Universities, 2013). Over and above, there is a challenge of overcrowded classrooms that university academics struggle with, resulting from failure to match increased students' enrolments with improved infrastructure. Consequently, teaching and learning environments are not conducive for quality learning and individual attention, which most students, especially those from poor socio-economic backgrounds, might desperately need.

Responses to Poor Student Performance

Several efforts have and are still being made at different levels to address the challenges related to student performance. For example, in August 2013, the CHE released a policy titled "A proposal for undergraduate curriculum reform in South Africa: A case for a flexible curriculum structure" (CHE, 2013a). In this report, it is argued that the HE system increased access without a proper plan of matching it with the parallel growth in the success and graduation rates of students. The CHE also noted that the existing extended curriculum programmes did not improve the success of all students. The CHE suggested key curriculum reforms that were based on four pillars: foundation provision, epistemic transitions, enhancement and enrichment. It is beyond the scope of this chapter to present the details of these pillars. For further reading, see CHE (2013a).

The DHET (2015) developed the Teaching Development Grant to assist universities to provide extra student support through tutorship, mentorship and through the implementation of the first-year experience programmes for students who needed it. This grant also helps lecturers to develop academic and research activities that potentially enhance teaching and learning. In addition, the HE South Africa's (HESA's) Working Group on Teaching and Learning was established to advise the HESA board on strategies to improve teaching and learning in HE. The Working Group made several recommendations aimed at enhancing teaching, learning and student success, including the implementation of a Teaching and Learning Charter as a measure for improving success rates (Malele, 2011).

In its efforts to assure quality in HE, the CHE (2014) introduced the Quality Enhancement Project (QEP), the aim of which is "to improve student success both at individual HEIs and in HE as a whole" (CHE, 2014, p. ii). The QEP also has a transformation agenda by which it seeks information from universities on how they address improvement of quality and success of poor students.

Some universities offer bridging courses and the National Benchmarking Tests (NBTs) as support programmes for mostly those students from disadvantaged backgrounds. Some concerns have been raised about NBTs being used as entry tests, which is not what it was meant for. Sosibo and Katiya (2015) report that universities make efforts to address students' academic challenges but claim that these efforts are fragmented and lack coherence and structure across and among different institutions. Clearly, therefore, there are efforts at various levels to address the parity between access and success for poor students.

With regard to infrastructural challenges, the DHET (2015) recommended the establishment of new campuses, the newest of which are the University of Mpumalanga in Mpumalanga Province, Sol Plaatjie University in the Northern Cape and Sefako Makgatho Health Sciences University in the North West Province. By increasing the number of universities, the DHET hopes to increase access as well. It is important for the DHET to consider that HWUs have, even during the apartheid era, had better infrastructure than HBUs. Therefore, a one-size-fits-all approach of improving infrastructure for all universities might not be the most ideal. The government should consider injecting more infrastructural funds to those universities that were marginalized by the apartheid system.

Regarding staffing and staff qualifications, the DHET has established the "Staffing South African Universities" Framework (SSAUF), which is mainly aimed at increasing young Black academics. One of the five programmes within this framework is the New Generation of Academics Programme (nGAP) aimed at recruiting and supporting a young generation of Black academics by providing them with a number of new and permanent posts at universities for a period of six years while they develop themselves. Other universities, such as Cape Peninsula University of Technology have developed the "Khula" project aimed at "growing their own timber" of students who obtained undergraduate degrees from them. Through this programme, universities employ and provide junior staff with minimal teaching workload so that they can complete master's and PhD degrees quicker. In addition, the National Research Foundation (NRF) works with universities to fast-track the production of master's and doctoral graduates by offering funds to staff to take sabbaticals and study leaves and to attend thesis-writing workshops.

In as far as colonized curriculum is concerned; debate on this issue is raging in all the South African universities. The aim is to dissect and get a better understanding of the concept of colonization so as to find a solution on how curriculum could be decolonized. Currently, there is no consensus on the meaning of this concept. Consequently, universities and students are working together to find a common ground from which to decolonize university curriculum. In addition, various universities are addressing calls for decolonizing university curriculum. An example of such efforts is the recent UCT Decolonial Winter School that took place on 24 to 30 June 2018, the goal of which was to disseminate knowledge on the pedagogy of praxis (critical pedagogy). Universities are also still seeking ways for addressing racism and the discriminatory university culture that permeate them.

Having said this, what has been particularly clear is that the wheel of transformation has been painfully slow and not much has been achieved (Nzimande, 2015b). Apparently, universities pay lip service to transformation. In the MOCR (2013, p. 1), "real and meaningful transformation is yet to be addressed."

Diminishing Financial Support for Higher Education

Several reasons explain the diminishing financial support for the South African HE system. Some emanate from the financial constraints caused by low socio-economic status of students (Cosser & Letseka, 2009); insufficient state funding in the form of the National Student Financial Aids Scheme (NSFAS), loans and scholarships (Badat, 2009); delays in the disbursement of state funds (Mabelebele, 2012) and mismanagement of the state funds earmarked for HE. These situations lead to students taking part-time jobs to supplement their meagre financial resources (Price, 2009), resulting in negative consequences for outputs and throughputs.

The government uses different funding formulae to support HE in SA. At the 2015 Summit, Nzimande reported that since its inception in 1999, the NSFAS had supported 1.5 million students, many of whom were the first generation to enter university education. The NSFAS is available as a federal loan to the financially needy tertiary students, which they are expected to pay back in instalments at a low interest rate upon completion of their studies. At that Summit, Nzimande (2015a) highlighted that the increases made available through NSFAS had been adversely affected by an increase in student tuition. The other challenge is mismanagement. Recently, the news of a female student who received an amount of R14,000,000.00 (R14m) instead of R1,400.00 at Walter Sisulu University went viral in the media (Breakey, 2017). Other problems are inexplicable delays in paying students, most of which relate to the mismanagement of funds.

Funza Lushaka is a bursary scheme for students who pursue degrees in teacher education and who specialize on scarce skill subjects such as mathematics and science (www.isasaschoolfinder.co.za/info/funza-lushaka-bursary-scheme/). Like NSFAS, Funza Lushaka funding has not proven to be well managed or to be enough to cater to the needs of all deserving students from poor financial backgrounds (Fengu, 2018). Unfortunately, as university tuition continues to rise, coupled with an alarming decline of HE government subsidy, students from low socio-economic backgrounds bear the brunt of being purged from the system. There are varying views on the government's handling of funding for HE in SA. Letseka and Maile (2008) believe mishandling of funds diminishes universities' contribution to social and economic development, which can lead to devastating effects for poor students.

The HESA (2014) concurs with Letseka and Maile, highlighting the alarming decline in HE government subsidy that results in universities being financially strapped. The current funding model for South African HE is such that block grants are given to universities on an equal basis. Consequently, a cost-sharing approach, as suggested by the Human Sciences Research Council's briefing, is used to fund universities (Mashatile, 2014). The basic idea is that universities are expected to raise third-stream income through, for example, student tuition fees, donations and research subsidy (including contract research). Nonetheless, there are concerns about this one-size-fits-all model, due to the debilitating effects of the apartheid system which resulted in predominantly HWUs being more capable to sustain themselves under the current model as a result of their higher research outputs compared to HBUs. Maimela (2015) avers that the former are also more capable to generate higher private-sector and donor incomes than the latter.

Failure of poor students to fund their education is another obstacle. This situation led to the #FeesMustFall campaign which had devastating effects, with some universities spending millions to repair the damaged buildings. Ironically, these effects forced some universities to hike the fees even further. Therefore, there were many gains made by protesting students in as far as cancelling the historical debt for a large number of students, as well as continued funding for those students who were in good standing academically. Nonetheless, the losses cannot be disregarded, as they, to a large extent, put a huge strain on the financial situation of the universities concerned.

Responses to Diminishing Financial Support
for Higher Education

In reaction to this challenge, the government committed to injecting more funds into the education system (DHET, 2015, p. 13). Shay (2016) mentions that from 2017 to 2020, the state has committed close to R1 billion (about US$71 million) per annum as "ear-marked" funding to support greater efficiency of teaching and learning. The purpose of these funds is to address the imperatives of equity and quality and to embrace the transformation of the education system. Nonetheless, these efforts are not enough. The government needs to consider that during and after the apartheid era, HBUs lagged behind their HWUs with regard to generating third-income stream, as pointed out earlier. Therefore, to distribute resources using a one-size-fits-all approach would be unfair. Government should inject more earmarked funding and grants for HBUs than for HWUs (Maimela, 2015). Maimela (2015) recommends the cancellation of the National Student Debt which currently runs in billions of Rands, as well as the continuation of low interest charges. The government has also embarked on converting final-year NSFAS loans to bursaries for students who successfully complete their final year of studies, which means that students only pay the loan of the years preceding their final year.

Universities responded differently to the #FeesMustFall campaign. Some, like the Free State University, raised funds to support financially stressed students. Similarly, in 2015 the University of Witwatersrand SRC embarked on a One Million Rand Campaign (Maimela, 2015). These initiatives provide good-practice examples from which other HEIs could learn. On the contrary, other universities reacted violently by bringing security companies to help maintain order while spending millions of Rands in the process. In some cases, violence bred violence as protesting students perceived the reaction by universities as a war against them.

An advanced step by the government to address funding challenges in the HE sector was the establishment of a Working Group in 2012 to advise the DHET minister on the feasibility of making education fee-free for poor students. In 2017, Jacob Zuma, the then president of South Africa, released the Fees Commission Report into the feasibility of free education. Findings of this commission revealed that the government was incapable of providing totally free education to students who are unable to finance their own education. For further reading on this matter, see Commission of Inquiry into HE and Training at www.justice.gov.za/commissions/FeesHET/index.html.

Conclusion

This chapter has shown that inequalities abound among university students and that they manifest themselves in the poor performance of students and diminishing financial support for HE. These conditions are more discernible among students from low socio-economic backgrounds than their privileged counterparts. This chapter has also shown that the remnants of the apartheid system have created differences in the experiences of students from different racial and socio-economic backgrounds. Consequently, the good that government and universities have done to address inequalities among students has been overshadowed by despair. Nevertheless, efforts by the government and universities to address inequalities among students from different backgrounds indicates that both are committed to embracing diversity and transformation in HE. This chapter has presented a number of policies, practices and initiatives aimed towards this cause. Nonetheless, more still needs to be done to expedite the transformation process and to ensure that all students benefit fully from the South African HE system and that teaching and learning occur in environments that embrace diversity. Only then will the country be able to produce human capital with a competitive edge to participate actively in the global marketplace.

Acknowledgement

I would like to acknowledge the NRF for the grant that allowed me to write and complete this book chapter.

References

Academy of Science of South Africa (ASSAF) Consensus Report. (2010). *The PhD Study: An Evidence-Based Study on How to Meet the Demands for High-Level Skills in an Emerging Economy*. Retrieved December 27, 2017 from www.assaf.org.za/files/2010/11/40696-Boldesign-PHD-small.pdf

Badat, M. S. (2009). Input from Vice-Chancellor Dr Hohammed Saleem Badat, Rhodes University. *Insight: Higher Education South Africa, 1*, 10–12.

Bozzoli, B. (2015). *Behind the University Funding Crisis*. Retrieved December 27, 2017 from www.politicsweb.co.za/news-and-analysis/behind-the-university-funding-crisis

Breakey, J. (2017). *NSFAS Sent a Student R14m, She Loses It by Going Viral*. Retrieved July 8, 2018 from https://memeburn.com/2017/08/nsfas-student-r14m-million-viral/

Conley, D. T. (2008). Rethinking college readiness. *New Directions for Higher Education, 144*, 3–13.

Cosser, M., & Letseka, M. (2009). Student retention and graduate destination: Higher education and labour market access and success. *Monograph*. Pretoria: Human Sciences Research Council.

Council on Higher Education. (2013a). *Vital stats 2011: Public higher education 2011*. Pretoria: Council for Higher Education.

Council on Higher Education. (2013b). *A proposal for undergraduate curriculum reform in South Africa: The case for a flexible curriculum structure* (Report of the Task Team on Undergraduate Curriculum Structure). Pretoria: Council on Higher Education.

Council on Higher Education. (2014). *Framework for institutional quality enhancement in the second period of quality assurance.* Pretoria: Institutional Audits Directorate, Council on Higher Education.

Council on Higher Education. (2015, October 15–17). *Transformation in higher education.* Discussion Paper Prepared for the Second National Higher Education Transformation Summit, 2015, Annexure 6. Second National Higher Education Summit. Inkosi Albert Luthuli International Conference Centre, Durban.

Department of Education. (1997). *Education White Paper 3: A Programme for the Transformation of Higher Education.* Department of Education, Pretoria.

Department of Higher Education and Training. (2013). *Report of the Working Group on Free University Education for the Poor in South Africa.* Higher Education & Training, Pretoria.

Department of Higher Education and Training. (2015, October 15–17). *Addressing systemic higher education transformation.* Department of Higher Education and Training Discussion. Paper Prepared for the Higher Education Transformation Summit held at the Inkosi Albert Luthuli International Conference Centre, Durban. Annexure 2. Second National Higher Education Summit. Inkosi Albert Luthuli International Conference Centre, Durban.

Du Preez, P., Simmonds, S., & Verhoef, A. H. (2016). Rethinking and researching transformation in higher education: A meta-study of South African trends. *Transformation in Higher Education, 1*(1), 1–7.

Fataar, A. (2017). *Decolonising education in South Africa: An interview with Aslam Fataar.* Retrieved from https://www.litnet.co.za/decolonising-education-south-africa-interview-aslam-fataar/

Fengu, M. (2018). *Bursary Scheme Fails as Students go Homeless.* Retrieved July 8, 2018 from https://city-press.news24.com/News/bursary-scheme-fails-as-students-go-homeless-20180501

Funza Lushaka Bursary Scheme, Finance for Teachers. Retrieved July 8, 2018 from www.isasaschoolfinder.co.za/info/funza-lushaka-bursary-scheme/

Higher Education South Africa. (2014). *Annual Report.* Retrieved from http://www.usaf.ac.za/wp-content/uploads/2016/09/HESA-Annual-report-2014-FINAL-LR.pdf

Jansen, J. (2017, November 30). "The problem with decolonisation": Jonathan Jansen seminar. In M. van Heerden (Ed.), *Stellenbosch University Seminar.* Retrieved December 27, 2017 from www.litnet.co.za/problem-decolonisation-jonathan-jansen-seminar/

Kraak, A. (2000). Changing modes: A brief overview of the mode 2 knowledge debate and its impact on South African policy formulation. In A. Kraak (Ed.), *Changing modes: New knowledge production and its implications for higher education in South Africa.* Pretoria: HSRC Press.

Le Grange, L. (2016). Decolonising the university curriculum. *South African Journal of Higher Education, 30*(2), 1–12.

Letseka, M. & Maile, S. (2008). *High university drop-out rates: A threat to South Africa's future*. Pretoria: HSRC Press.

Mabelebele, J. (2012, May 5). *Towards strengthening HESA-NASDEV partnerships: Some tentative views*. Keynote Address, National Association of Student Development Practitioners, Johannesburg, Emperors' Palace.

Maimela. D. (2015, October 15–17). *South African higher education transformation: What is to be done?* A Working Paper on Key Policy Issues from a Student Movement Perspective, Prepared for the Second National Higher Education Transformation Summit held at the Inkosi Albert Luthuli International Conference Centre, Durban. Annexure 16. Second National Higher Education Summit. Inkosi Albert Luthuli International Conference Centre, Durban.

Malele, I. (2011). *Access to Higher Education: Challenges: Higher Education SA Briefing Higher Education and Training*. Retrieved December 13, 2017 from https://pmg.org.za/committee-meeting/12495/

Mashatile, P. (2014). *Status & Effectiveness of Student Funding: DHET, NSFAS, HESA; FFC, HSRC & Stats SA Briefings: Standing Committee on Appropriations*. Retrieved November 31, 2017 from https://pmg.org.za/committee-meeting/17701/

The Ministerial Oversight Committee on Transformation in South African Public Universities. (2013, October 15–17). *The transformation of South African higher education*. Concept Paper Prepared for the Second National Higher Education Transformation Summit Held at the Inkosi Albert Luthuli International Conference Centre, Durban. Annexure 8. Second National Higher Education Summit. Inkosi Albert Luthuli International Conference Centre, Durban.

National Planning Commission. (2012). Our future-make it work: National Development Plan 2030. Retrieved from https://www.poa.gov.za/news/Documents/NPC%20National%20Development%20Plan%20Vision%202030%20-lo-res.pdf

Nzimande, B. (2015a, October 15–17). Speech by Minister of Blade Nzimande at the 2nd National Higher Education Transformation Summit Held at the Inkosi Albert Luthuli International Conference Centre, Durban. Retrieved December 26, 2017 from www.gov.za/speeches/speech-minister-be-nzimande-higher-education-summit-held-inkosi-albert-luthuli-icc-durban

Nzimande, B. (2015b, January 15). *Transformation of South African universities too slow*. Speech by Minister of Blade Nzimande at the Education Alliance Meeting, University of Johannesburg. Retrieved December 27, 2017 from www.engineeringnews.co.za/article/transformation-of-south-african-universities-too-slow-nzimande-2015-01-16

Patrinos, H. A. (2016). *Why Education Matters for Economic Development*. Retrieved December 28, 2017 from http://blogs.worldbank.org/education/why-education-matters-economic-development

Price, M. (2009). Input from Vice-Chancellor Dr. Max Price, University of Cape Town. *Insight*, *1*, 26–27.

Schreiner, L., & Hulme, E. (2009). Assessment of students' strengths and the first step to student success. In B. Leibowitz, A. Van der Merwe, & S. Van Schalkwyk (Eds.), *Focus on first-year success: Perspectives emerging from South Africa and beyond* (pp. 69–78). Stellenbosch: Sun Press.

Shay, S. (2016). Four scenarios for higher education in South Africa. *The Conversation*. Retrieved December 23, 2017 from https://businesstech.co.za/news/lifestyle/132607/four-scenarios-for-higher-education-in-south-africa/

Sosibo, Z., & Katiya, M. (2015). Closing the loop between access and success: Early identification of at-risk students and monitoring as key strategies used by a South African university. *International Journal of Educational Sciences*, 8(2), 271–279.

Universities South Africa. (2015, October 15–17). *Reflections on higher education transformation.* Discussion paper Prepared for the Second national Higher Education Transformation Summit Held at the Inkosi Albert Luthuli International Conference Centre, Durban. Annexure 8. Second National Higher Education Summit. Inkosi Albert Luthuli International Conference Centre, Durban.

Wanjohi, A. M. (2011). *Integral Education for Social-Economic Development in Africa.* KENPRO Online Papers Portal. Retrieved December 28, 2017 from www. kenpro.org/papers

Wilson-Strydom, M. (2015, October 15–17). *Access and success-transitions into and through higher education.* Briefing Paper Prepared for the Second National Higher Education Transformation Summit Held at the Inkosi Albert Luthuli International Conference Centre, Durban. Annexure 12. Second National Education Summit. Inkosi Albert Luthuli International Conference Centre, Durban.

Theme 4

What strategies have been introduced or could be introduced at Cape Peninsula University of Technology in Cape Town, South Africa, to create and advance support for quality research and teaching that benefits the demographic composition of South African academics and students, and the needs of the South African multicultural society?

5 "They Don't Leave Any Room for Humanity; Yet, They Expect You to Be Humane"

Cape Town Teachers' Responses to the Curriculum Assessment Policy Statements (CAPS)

Kristian Stewart and Eunice N. Ivala

Introduction

This chapter explores a digital storytelling classroom activity in a senior phase education course at Cape Peninsula University of Technology. Teacher education students spent eight weeks participating in a digital storytelling unit meant to teach them how to communicate with diverse learners across varied sociocultural and historical contexts. Framed by literature stemming from the turn of higher education (HE) after the onset of democracy in South Africa (SA), the sustainability of the digital storytelling project was questioned with an interest in, if the students carried this knowledge from the university classroom into their teaching practices.

Transforming Higher Education and Curriculum Standards: Post-Apartheid

With apartheid's end, institutions of HE required distinct and specific measures of reorganization. Up until 1994, demarcated schooling systems were education's defining characteristic. The HE Act of 1997 formed the Council on Higher Education (CHE) to address the transitioning educational climate. In *Education White Paper 3: A Programme for the Transformation of Higher Education*, the Council (1997b) outlined a programme for HE that would forward a democratic vision based on redressing past inequities and responding to a new social order. The CHE's (2000) successive report provided an additional framework to reconfigure HE as it moved fully into the 21st century.

The Department of Education (2001) instructed all schools to be governed by the ten guiding principles as mentioned in the 1996 Constitution. These guiding principles included social justice and equity, equality, non-racism and non-sexism, ubuntu (human dignity), an open society, accountability (responsibility), the rule of law, respect, and reconciliation. The "Norms and Standards for Educators" (2000) highlighted seven parameters under which teachers should be trained, emphasizing democratic values, integration, and nurturing equality. However, The Norms and Standards were replaced by the "Minimum Requirements for Teacher Education Qualifications" in 2010, which was authored by the Department of Higher Education and Training (DHET). The DHET recognized that many teacher preparatory programmes lacked minimum curriculum standards, did not prepare students appropriately, and did not believe that all university programmes understood the depth of challenges facing education in SA. Additionally, the Norms and Standards for Educators described the attributes an effective teacher should be able to demonstrate. In part, the standards endorsed a "critical, committed, and ethical attitude towards developing a sense of respect and responsibility towards others" adjacent to how teachers should "promote democratic values and practices in schools and society by means of developing supportive and empowering learning environments" (p. 4). Last, the Norms and Standards state, "Teacher education programmes must incorporate situational and contextual elements that assist teachers to develop competences to enable them to deal with diversity and transformation" (p. 7).

The guidelines on restructuring HE (and education more broadly) would mean students preparing to become teachers would have to turn into national curriculum experts, even though curriculum in SA's public schools since the advent of democracy has been constantly in flux. To start, a national curriculum was established in 1998, which was an outcome-based education (OBE) system titled "Curriculum 2005." In 2005, Curriculum 2005 was renamed the National Curriculum Statement. The National Curriculum Statement was amended in 2009 to include the Curriculum and Assessment Policy Statements (CAPS). Pearson SA (Variend, 2011) has defined CAPS as an extensive curricular outline where "every subject in each grade will have a single, comprehensive and concise policy document that will provide details on what teachers need to teach and assess on a grade-by-grade and subject-by-subject basis" (para. 1). CAPS was implemented on a rolling basis between 2012 to 2014, and Pearson has written the application of CAPS's was expected to improve educational quality and to provide clear and consistent expectations on classroom instruction. A foregrounding tenant of CAPS is its centralized curriculum, unified across each grade level and subject, applied to every school in SA. As a curriculum arrangement, CAPS draws from van den Akker's (2010) macro, meso, and nano distinctions as CAPS places emphasis on education in both the nation/state (macro), the school/institution that executes the lesson plans (meso), and the personal (nano) with a focus on learner diversity and inclusion.

However, despite these changes, the chaotic nature associated with revolutionizing SA's curriculum has led to teacher overload, stress, and turmoil (Adu & Ngibe, 2014). Adu and Ngibe (2014) have cited the confusion teachers have faced in adhering to curriculum standards that constantly change, while du Plessis and Marais (2015) have explained CAPS as a curriculum of "what to teach" versus methodology or "how to teach" (para. 1), where "teachers have little say in what they teach and when" (para. 50). The teachers taking part in a study conducted by Pasha, Bipath, and Beckmann (2016) deemed the prescribed CAPS curriculum useful, but they also felt ill prepared and unable to properly execute the curriculum. A study conducted by Maharajh, Nkosi, and Mkhize (2016), examining teacher experiences as they integrated CAPS, exposed CAPS as filled with challenges but also that the education sector was equally plagued with difficulties. Maharajh, Nkosi, and Mkhizi attributed these challenges to lack of material resources and poor teacher training. As Khoza (2015) explored teacher experiences with the CAPS curriculum, data revealed the teachers in his study did not understand curriculum theories that serve as a foundation for the policy statements. What this body of work reveals is a need to further interrogate the gaps between preparing teacher educators and strategies for effective CAPS integration and classroom applications.

Research Objective and Research Questions

To explore digital storytelling and its usefulness as a learning activity and as a pedagogy for future classroom teachers, a case study (Creswell, 2009) was implemented in a teacher education course at a large university of technology in the Western Cape of SA during the 2014–2015 academic year.

This study was framed by the following questions:

1. Have students integrated digital storytelling into their classrooms or curriculum as first-year teachers?
2. How are students appropriating the digital storytelling process after the completion of the course?

Research Design and Methodology

Case study (Creswell, 2009) and ethnographic inquiry (Clifford, 1980), both derived from the qualitative research paradigm, were selected as a research practice for this study, whose data is presented in this chapter. The qualitative research paradigm privileges lived experiences and face-to-face interactions and values the environment of the subjects under study. Scholars working in the area of qualitative research articulate the importance of making the site of study visible to the observer in order to make sense of the meanings people bring to a phenomenon (Denzin & Lincoln, 2005). Working over an extended period with the students, interviewing them on multiple occasions, and visiting their classrooms aided the understanding of the questions being posed and allowed the researcher to better understand the phenomenon or "case" under study via participant observation (Stake, 1995, p. 2).

Sampling

The participants in this study ($n = 9$) were enrolled in a course titled Professional Studies. The participants volunteered to be small-group facilitators for the larger Professional Studies ($N = 67$) course before the start of the term. The participants can be characterized as a convenience sample (Creswell, 2009) because students made themselves available by volunteering. The participants were both men and women and represented the racial categories (Black African, Coloured, and White) existing in SA. Students in the Professional Studies course were tasked with creating a digital story as part of a teaching portfolio, and the participant/facilitators led small groups of students through this process. Professional Studies is the last course students take before graduating with degrees in Education (BEd General Education and Training or BEd Intermediate and Senior Phases). This study was included in a larger dissertation project (Stewart, 2016), received institutional ethical clearance, all participants signed waivers of consent, and participant names have been altered to protect their identity.

Data Generation and Analysis

The data presented here include interviews (ethnographic; Spradley, 1979) on three occasions with the facilitators, classroom visits, and researcher field notes. Interviews were conducted during the term (participants were students) and then twice after the class ended when students held teaching positions in and around the Western Cape. Spradley's (1979) concept of an ethnographic interview—taking place on multiple occasions and over time to develop trust between the researcher and subjects—is an accurate way to characterize these interactions. Formal interviews (with specific questions) lasted from 30 minutes to over an hour, depending on the student, and interviews were recorded before being transcribed into scripts to maintain veracity. However, impromptu talks with the participants before and after class, during lunch, and even on the weekends were documented in the researcher's field notes applying both thin and thick descriptive measures to the note-taking (Geertz, 1973). Classroom visits were by student invitation and lasted anywhere from a few hours to the entire school day. Analytical and descriptive field notes were authored throughout the duration of this study.

Data were analyzed by applying Saldaña's (2012) method of coding qualitative research to understand the nature of the aggregate data. During the first round of analysis, "In-Vivo" coding was applied to the transcripts and field notes. In-Vivo coding, described by Saldaña, is the process of looking for literal words and actual participant language in the data record. Focused (and Axial) coding was then utilized to arrange the emergent themes into categories. Validity was ensured by the triangulation and cross-referencing of multiple research methods across the varied data points. Direct quotes and phrases are provided in this chapter to certify the reliability of the research process and to honor the participants' voices.

The Digital Storytelling Project

Digital stories are audiovisual compositions that merge music and images alongside each student's voice as the overarching narration (Lambert, 2012). In the Professional Studies course, students were required to create a digital story on a critical aspect of education as a final component of their teaching portfolio. As students shared their narratives (complete with hand-drawn illustrations detailing their lives until that moment), they were positioned to bear witness to the stories and experiences of the people around them. Next, students penned and edited these narratives before shaping them into a digital story via media software for Windows. Once completed, the students screened their digital stories in a public forum at the end of the term. Digital storytelling encourages students to openly share stories, to build trust while doing so, and to engage across difference. In the Professional Studies context, digital storytelling was applied as a socializing pedagogy, and integrated learners who remained segregated despite SA's efforts to transform educational spaces. There is a wide body of literature that supports the use of digital storytelling both as a practice in HE and for the purposes of training teachers (Chigona et al., 2013; Fletcher & Cambre, 2009; Gachago, Ivala, Condy, & Chigona, 2013; Stewart, 2017; Stewart & Ivala, 2017).

Findings

CAPS and the Creation of Oppressive Teaching Environments

When the students (as teachers) were asked if they carried over any of the concepts they learned in the Professional Studies course into their teaching practices, they expressed frustration regarding the strict CAPS curriculum requirements that left them unable to write their own lesson plans or to interject innovative teaching strategies within their classrooms. Students labeled the national curriculum "impossible," "without depth," and "cruel."

Furthermore, all the students clearly stated they felt "oppressed" under the CAPS curriculum and explained how they had little to no independence as teachers, how some were given CAPS approved lesson plans, and how they were heavily regulated to make sure CAPS was explicitly followed. Per the students, there could be no deviation from the established CAPS curriculum.

Overwhelmingly, students commented on their dislike of CAPS and their belief that it lacked both autonomy and academic rigor. Felix reported, "I don't like CAPS at all. It's not only that it is too restrictive, it's too shallow. It has no depth, no substance." Andre, in his interview, shared how CAPS did not address the social issues the Constitution requires. He said, "We forget about the holistic learning. CAPS doesn't prepare you to deal with social problems. CAPS is one click." Andre also labeled CAPS as "dangerous ground" as, in his opinion, CAPS dropped learning standards, rather than raising them. In fact, Andre said SA should lower its flag as a complement to SA's low standards of education. Graeme added this sentiment regarding CAPS: "CAPS does not let us think out of the box or be innovative. It wants us to be robots because they want to control what we teach the kids."

Andre and Tayla both spoke to the challenges of implementing CAPS due to large class sizes and the amount of work required to maintain CAPS records. Many of the teachers stated how they were tasked with writing and preparing the lesson plans for other teachers in their same subject and grade-level areas. They also reported in some of the subjects they instruct how they are not allowed to write their own lesson plans. Rather, plans are drafted for them by department heads to ensure they are CAPS aligned. The teachers who crafted lesson plans for their colleagues stated how they were forced to omit creative or technically savvy pedagogical approaches in order to keep plans simple and usable for any teacher and audience.

In the response to the workload required to maintain CAPS, one student mentioned enlisting the help of a boyfriend to grade papers. Another communicated how he was forced to work throughout the weekend just to keep up with the report writing. Luniko shared during his interview that he would quit the profession if he was not so strong due to the workload. Andre also labored to write plans for other teachers, but his primary concern was how to educate the 47 students in his class since 17 of them were grade repeaters. Classroom management and remedial tutorials took up most of his time, adjacent to CAPS, and left him no time for the care he wished to give his class or a space to develop the varied teaching strategies he learned as a university student.

Being a Parachute: The Case of Tayla

In the follow-up interviews, when the students held teaching appointments, questions were raised to assess how students incorporated digital storytelling into their classrooms. Rather than answering the question outright, Tayla shared an anecdote about having to attend a professional development workshop called "Disciplining With Courage." Tayla conveyed how she struggled to take this workshop seriously due to the demands of teaching, staying true to the CAPS curriculum, and positively impacting students with special needs who are integrated into her classroom without support. Tayla shared:

> [A]nd the principle tells us, "You have to be this child's parachute. He's falling! You have to catch him!" I am thinking kids that come from broken homes, social issues . . . disruptive kids. So, I asked my principal, "How do I complete my curriculum? How am I all off these things at the same time?" So, my answer to you is . . . it is almost impossible for me to incorporate that [digital storytelling] into my class . . . with all that I need to cover. . . . They expect you to be a parachute, but they don't leave room for it in the curriculum.

Tayla additionally shared an example of her increased empathy with a "problem student," one that other teachers had given up on. She expressed that she would not be able to help this student until he trusted her enough to share his story. Tayla described this student as a frequent troublemaker, and she shared how another teacher asked her why she did not simply "lose it" and just "yell at him." Tayla replied to the teacher how she wanted to listen to this student when he acted up. She went on to say,

> So even though he does this and I should be very angry at him, I am not . . . because I don't know his story. There is *something* [emphasis hers]. He needs time to trust me. But there is no room in the CAPS to get that story in there. . . . You won't get through to them [students] and understand them if you don't know their stories.

Better Human Skills

In follow-up interviews, the teachers reported how the project ignited feelings of empathy and concern toward others that they did not feel before they participated in the digital storytelling project. Students utilized this skill set both inside and outside of the classroom as they worked to build relationships with their students and to embrace more meaningful communication patterns with their peers, neighbors, and coworkers. Overall, the students, now teachers, touted the benefits of the project. They related how although they were not integrating the technical and critical media skills from the digital storytelling project into their classrooms, they did carry over a desire to share and to listen to stories as a result of the storytelling process. Andre stated how post-project he became a conscientious listener when bearing witness to the social problems his students brought with them to class. Mia stated that it was important to create a space for her students to "let their stories out," even though the curriculum has left her little time to do so. Pieter shared how he used the participatory learning activity he learned from the digital storytelling project to teach poetry. Luniko was inspired by this project and included stories of the xenophobic attacks on immigrants that plagued SA at the time in his classroom, even though he felt he was "cheating" on the curriculum to do so.

Outside of the classroom, Tayla claimed that her awareness of *how* she listened transitioned from the beginning to the end of the project. She shared, "Before you would hear, but don't listen. But now I listen *and* hear." Tayla used this to illustrate how the digital storytelling project, in her words, "changed people" and made the participants more willing to communicate with people external of their comfort zones long after the project ended. Mia also had a positive response regarding the aftermath of the project. She was very clear that she now wished to widen her social circle and to get closer to other people. For Mia, this was an important statement because she was both incredibly guarded and had not mixed with people outside of her race until attending university. Graeme reported how he created, in his words, a "proper human connection" with a student (of a different ethnicity) from the course that would not have been possible if not for the storytelling.

Felix, Rob, and Luniko distributed their digital storytelling experiences within their social groups and applied what they learned in the context of their daily lives. Felix shared his story of drug rehabilitation with people from his past in an effort for them to understand that they, too, could modify the course of their lives. As Felix expressed, "I showed some of my old friends the story and they were really impressed. 'Wow . . . anybody can change if they really want to.'"

Rob described how the project taught him how to be "open to listening." He shared examples of how he applied this new-found skill with his colleagues at work. Rob also noted becoming more empathetic toward a neighbor that he was not so friendly with before the project. Rob stated that he "didn't know her story" but now was inspired to learn more about her. Rob additionally brought up the xenophobic attacks that were ongoing in SA at the time and expressed that nobody was listening to the stories of the people being targeted and abused. Most importantly, Rob clearly stated that he did not care in this same way before the project.

When Luniko was questioned if he was using any part of the digital storytelling project since the completion of his university class, he replied:

> Yes. With my friends and at social gatherings, I always tell my friends about the digital storytelling and how the people of SA can walk with pride with their untold stories. I was just telling my friend how the project

was healing and how it was good to hear from what other people had to say about their lives . . . and how good it was just to sit and listen to other people's stories because actually it was teaching you as a person to learn to listen and to just give other people their space . . . to express themselves and share the power of listening.

Additionally, due to lack of technology and material resources, students could not implement the digital storytelling project as first-year teachers in the way they experienced it in the university classroom. Furthermore, classroom observations revealed a lack of technology (access to and materiality of) at every school that was visited. As examples, Mia's school had no Internet services or computers. If she wished to share a web-based activity with her students, she had to bring in her own computer to do so. Andre's school had one computer lab, but it was reserved solely for math instruction and could only be entered via a security code. Lack of material resources, coupled with strict curricular mandates, left teachers with little autonomy and choice but to use the supplies provided by the schools. Therefore, there is merit in questing the validity of an eight-week university project that relies heavily on technology considering teachers cannot replicate such a learning scenario at local schools. This is key if the goal of such a project is to instruct future teachers on to how they might integrate a media literacy project into their pedagogical approaches.

The disconnect teachers described between transitioning their university education into their teaching praxes is also a conclusion Khoza (2015) discovered when he examined postgraduate student teachers and their implementation of CAPS. Khoza found the student teachers were unable to interpret the curriculum because they lacked the theoretical knowledge necessary to understand CAPS. This study complements Khoza's conclusions by also revealing a gap between the teachers' university education and their teaching practices, which is an area that requires future examination. To provide a linkage to CAPS, the Professional Studies class could have highlighted how digital storytelling can be centered around the development of critical writing skills, as no matter the content area, effective writing is valued across the curriculum. Emphasizing literacy might have alleviated Felix's concerns about generating written statements and provided a way for him to bridge the digital storytelling project to CAPS. Establishing a relationship between the digital storytelling assignment (and other university assignments) to CAPS subject area outcomes could serve to mitigate a critique of CAPS as being only what to teach, not how to teach it (du Plessis & Marais, 2015). Future research could center around what the students in this study found beneficial about the digital storytelling process (listening and relationship building) and how they might develop classroom strategies that join those benefits to specific CAPS learning objectives.

Concluding Remarks: (Re)Storying the Curriculum

A major directive of the National Curriculum Statement (NCS) addresses educational inequities through the implementation of a standardized curriculum. CAPS, as an addition to the NCS, offers a detailed outline of how instructional time should be spent in relation to guiding teachers in what items should be assessed. CAPS does not, as the teachers mentioned, afford room for educators to connect with students on an affective or human level. According to the Department of Basic Education (2015), the curriculum aims to value knowledge systems and the rich histories of students and it is "sensitive to issues of diversity" (para. 3). CAPS also requires students to develop a sense of responsibility to others through supportive learning environments. However, prohibiting teachers to instruct the curriculum in a way that responds to the needs of their distinct classrooms hampers trust-building efforts and devalues the important work of teachers. Furthermore, Sayed explained in 2004 how teacher training became removed from the emancipatory rhetoric found in the anti-apartheid struggle. Seemingly, CAPS and the NCS are working in opposition to the goals set by the Department of Basic Education to tackle issues surrounding social transformation. Furthermore, if teachers are unable to humanize their teaching practices how might they develop the competencies needed to enable them to effectively deal with diversity and transformation as the Norms and Standards for Educators (2000) dictates?

According to the participants in this study, the national curriculum that, in part, is meant to support engagement across difference leaves little room for its actual inclusion in classroom practice. Projects like the digital storytelling assignment created a humanizing classroom space to examine both the "self" and "other," as students worked toward unpacking the lines that divided them. If a goal of South African school-sponsored curriculum is to create racial equity, then learning activities that promote empathy should not only be used in public classrooms but should also be deeply embedded in the curriculum at all levels of education. The teachers who participated in the digital storytelling project viewed effective teaching as grounded in getting to know their students, through storytelling and sharing—skills they developed in their Professional Studies course. The teachers also took these skills outside of the classroom walls by becoming more interested and caring to the people in their lives, whether these people already existed in their social circles (like Luniko) or they were strangers in the news as in Rob's case. In SA, creating a curriculum of care by grounding all classroom activities within the frameworks of compassion and respect for others should be considered as highly prized as a curriculum of basic skills. Fragmented relationships are apartheid's sustaining legacy. Education has a duty to make repairs in this area as well. We argue that projects like digital storytelling that emphasize better human skills can lead to improved relationship building and teaching skills—and with that a reimagined SA.

References

Adu, E. O., & Ngibe, N. C. P. (2014). Continuous change in curriculum: South African teachers' perceptions. *Mediterranean Journal of Social Sciences, 5*(23), 983–989. Retrieved from www.mcser.org/journal/index.php/mjss/article/viewFile/4617/4482

Chigona, A., Condy, J., Ivala, E. & Gachago, D. (2013). Digital Storytelling in a pre-service teachers' classroom: A Community of Practice. Society for Information Technology & Teacher Education International Conference (pp. 1491–1498). Association for the Advancement of Computing in Education (AACE). Retrieved from https://scholar.google.co.za/citations?user=Yr1ZitgAAAAJ&hl=en#d=gs_md_cita-d&u=%2Fcitations%3Fview_op%3Dview_citation%26hl%3Den%26user%3DYr1ZitgAAAAJ%26cstart%3D20%26pagesize%3D80%26citation_for_view%3DYr1ZitgAAAAJ%3ATyk-4Ss8FVUC%26tzom%3D-120

Clifford, J. (1980). Fieldwork, reciprocity, and the making of ethnographic texts: The example of Maurice Leenhardt. *Royal Anthropological Institute of Great Britain and Ireland, 15*(3), 518–532. Retrieved from www.jstor.org/stable/2801348

Council on Higher Education South Africa. (1997a, January). *Higher Education Act 101 of 1997.* Retrieved from www.che.ac.za/media_and_publications/legislation/higher-education-act-101-1997

Council on Higher Education South Africa. (1997b, July). *Education White Paper: A Programme for the Transformation of Higher Education.* Retrieved from www.che.ac.za/media_and_publications/legislation/education-white-paper-3-programme-transformation-higher-education

Council on Higher Education South Africa. (2000). *Towards a New Higher Education Landscape: Meeting the Equity, Quality and Social Development Imperatives of South Africa in the 21st Century.* Size and Shape of Higher Education Task Team. Retrieved from https://www.che.ac.za/sites/default/files/publications/New_HE_Landscape.pdf

Creswell, J. W. (2009). *Research design: Qualitative, quantitative, and mixed methods approaches* (3rd ed.). Thousand Oaks, CA: Sage Publications.

Denzin, N. K., & Lincoln, Y. S. (2005). *The Sage handbook of qualitative research* (3rd ed.). Thousand Oaks, CA: Sage Publications.

Department of Basic Education Republic South Africa. (2015). *Curriculum Assessment Policy Statements.* Retrieved from www.education.gov.za/Curriculum/NCSGrades R12/CAPS/tabid/420/Default.aspx

Department of Education. (2000). Norms and standards for educators. *Government Gazette, 415*(20844). Retrieved from http://us-cdn.creamermedia.co.za/assets/articles/attachments/08137_notice82.pdf

Department of Education. (2001). *Manifesto on Values, Education and Democracy.* Retrieved from www.education.gov.za/LinkClick.aspx?fileticket=tYzHKQLJLJE%3D&tabid=129&mid=425

Du Plessis, E., & Marais, P. (2015). *Reflections on the NCS to NCS (CAPS): Foundation Phase Teachers' Experiences.* Retrieved from http://iiespace.iie.ac.za/bitstream/handle/11622/59/Reflections.pdf?sequence=1

Fletcher, C., & Cambre, C. (2009). Digital storytelling and implicated scholarship in the classroom. *Journal of Canadian Studies, 43*(1), 109–130. Retrieved from www.academia.edu/185633/Digital_storytelling_and_implicated_scholarship_in_the_classroom

Gachago, D., Ivala, E., Condy, J., & Chigona, A. (2013). Journeys across difference: Preservice teacher education students' perceptions of a pedagogy of discomfort in a digital storytelling project in South Africa. *Critical Studies in Teaching and Learning, 1*(1), 22–52. doi:10.14426/cristal.v1i1.4

Geertz, C. (1973). *The interpretation of cultures.* New York, NY: Basic Books.

Khoza, S. B. (2015). Student teachers' reflections on their practices of the Curriculum and Assessment Policy Statement. *South African Journal of Higher Education, 29*(4), 179–197. Retrieved from http://hdl.handle.net/10520/EJC182450

Lambert, J. (2012). *Digital storytelling: Capturing lives, creating community* (4th ed.). London, UK: Routledge.

Maharajh, L.R., Nkosi, T., & Mkhize, M.C. (2016). Teachers' Experiences of the Implementation of the Curriculum and Assessment Policy Statement (CAPS) in Three Primary Schools in KwaZulu Natal. *Africa's Public Service Delivery & Performance Review, 4*(3), a120. doi: https://doi.org/10.4102/apsdpr.v4i3.120

Phasha, T., Bipath, K., & Beckmann, J. (2016). Teachers' Experiences Regarding Continuous Professional Development and the Curriculum Assessment Policy Statement. *International Journal of Educational Sciences, 14*(1–2), 69–78. doi: 10.1080/09751122.2016.11890480

Saldaña, J. (2012). *The coding manual for qualitative researchers* (2nd ed.). Thousand Oaks, CA: Sage Publications.

Sayed, Y. (2004). The case of teacher education in post-apartheid South Africa: Politics and priorities. In L. Chisholm (Ed.), *Changing class: Education and social change in post-apartheid South Africa* (pp. 247–276). Cape Town, South Africa: HSRC Press.

Spradley, J. (1979). *The ethnographic interview.* New York, NY: Holt, Reinhart, & Winston.

Stake, R. (1995). *The art of case study research.* Thousand Oaks, CA: Sage Publications.

Stewart, K. D. (2016). *What's left unsaid: Rewriting and restorying in a South African teacher education classroom* (Doctoral dissertation). Retrieved from DEEP BLUE Database at the University of Michigan http://hdl.handle.net/2027.42/118196

Stewart, K. D. (2017). Classrooms as "safe houses"? The ethical and emotional implications of digital storytelling in a university writing classroom. *Critical Studies in Teaching and Learning (CriSTaL), [S.l.], 5*(1), 85–102. Retrieved from http://cristal.epubs.ac.za/index.php/cristal/article/view/102

Stewart, K. D., & Ivala, E. (2017). Silence, voice, and "other languages": Digital storytelling as a site for resistance and restoration in a South African higher education classroom. *British Journal of Educational Technology, 48*(5), 1164–1175. doi:10.1111/bjet.12540

van den Akker, J. (2010). Building bridges: How research may improve curriculum policies and classroom practices. In S. Stoney (Ed.), *Beyond Lisbon 2010: Prospective from research and development for education policy in Europe* (pp. 175–195). CIDEE, Consortium of Institutions for Development and Research in Education in Europe. Sint-Katelijne-Waver, Belgium.

Variend, A. (2011). *What Is "CAPS"?* Retrieved from http://maskewmillerlongman.ning.com/profiles/blogs/what-you-need-to-know-about

Theme 5

What new institutional identities have been developed or could be developed by a merged university like Cape Peninsula University of Technology in Cape Town, South Africa, to rise above preceding apartheid injustices?

6 Diverse Staff Voices on the Transformation of a Merged South African University of Technology

Eunice N. Ivala, Daniela Gachago and Zilungile Sosibo

Introduction

More than a decade has passed since the incorporations and mergers of institutions of higher education in South Africa. These mergers were aimed at creating institutions with new identities and cultures consistent with the vision, values and principles of non-racial and non-sexist democratic society and transformation of higher education institutions into effective and efficient institutions that are responsive and contribute to the changing intellectual skills and knowledge of South Africa (Seepe, 2010). Yet there is little literature or documentation on the mergers, outcomes and lessons learnt (Hay & Fourie, 2002; Seepe, 2010).

This chapter presents staff experiences of the merger and transformation processes and outcomes, and lessons learnt at the Cape Peninsula University of Technology (CPUT), the largest institution of higher learning in the Western Cape. The purpose is to allow the institution to measure the outcomes of the merger, identify lessons learnt and plan ways of improving on whatever merger goals have not been achieved. Furthermore, understanding the outcomes of the mergers and the lessons learnt will enable other institutions to design relevant interventions to advance the transformation of institutions and to address any concerns that may have arisen as a result of the mergers. The chapter is informed by Archer's social realism model (1995, 1996, 1998). Data were gathered during four digital storytelling workshops held in 2013 and 2014 with academics and administration staff. The River of Life, a visual brainstorming technique, and the story circle, in which participants shared their stories, were used to gather data presented in this chapter. These two are key stages of the digital storytelling process (Lambert, 2009), which will be described in more detail in the chapter and where the digital stories are shared and co-created among participants. Data were analysed deductively by mapping issues arising from the data on Archer's social realism model elements. The conclusion and recommendations for the institution on how to support transformation close this chapter.

Theoretical Framework: Archer's Social Realism

Archer's social realism model (1995, 1996, 1998) provides a model of social reality as comprising three milieus: structural, cultural and agentic. The structural milieu includes things that exist such as policies and committees, as well as more abstract phenomena such as race, gender, social class and knowledge structures, in the higher education system. The cultural milieu speaks to how and what we think about things. This includes our values, beliefs, attitudes and ideologies. The agentic milieu refers to people. Various logics underpin culture, structure and agency and these can be complementary or contradictory. While all three are always at play in the social world, they may differ in the extent of their conditioning influence at any given time.

Digital Storytelling, Story Circle and the "River of Life"

The study was influenced by the digital storytelling model developed by the StoryCenter in Berkeley, California. Originating from a history of critical theatre, the StoryCenter digital storytelling model has as its main objective to fight for social justice by giving marginalized groups a voice. On its website,[1] the StoryCenter explains what the sharing of stories means:

> Personal narratives can touch viewers deeply, moving them to reflect on their own experiences, modify their behavior, treat others with greater compassion, speak out about injustice, and become involved in civic and political life. Whether online, in social media or local communities, or at the institutional/policy level, the sharing of stories has the power to make a real difference.

Figure 6.1 River of Life

Figure 6.2 The Story Circle

The StoryCenter showcases many stories from marginalized groups who are often silenced through the hegemony of public discourses. At the core of their stories is an "act of self-discovery, and a means to localize and control the context of their presentation" (Lambert, 2009, p. 82). Foregrounding the communal sharing of stories, the StoryCenter sees digital storytelling not as an individual process, but as a collective process of developing stories in what they call the "story circle" (see Figure 6.2) (Lambert, 2010). Their model of creating digital stories is quite specific and involves a workshop running over several days, in which participants collaboratively develop their stories. The communal sharing of stories in the story circle is the main element in the process of digital storytelling (Lambert, 2010, p. v).

For this study the digital storytelling workshop as developed by the Story-Center was slightly adapted. As participants had to negotiate high workloads and many responsibilities, the workshop was limited to one day, where lecturers and administration staff shared their stories of the merger and transformation in a story circle. The digital story was developed in follow-up sessions on a one-to-one basis as a collaboration between the participant and digital storytelling facilitators. To start of the process of story sharing, which can often be difficult and daring, we introduced a participatory learning and action (PLA) technique, the "River of Life" (see Figure 6.1). Participatory learning and action techniques, such as Community Maps or the River of Life, are open-ended, flexible, visual learning methods that allow participants with diverse academic literacy backgrounds to explore how they have been placed "in relation to resources and the privilege and harm emerging from their positioning in relation to resources in the light of their own experiences" (Bozalek, 2011, p. 475) and dialogue. These techniques can promote critical reflection regarding the social arrangements of inequality and privilege (ibid). Of particular importance is the collaborative interaction PLA techniques provide for differently positioned participants to share their perspectives and begin to engage with each other (Bozalek & Biersteker, 2010, p. 554).

We found these activities useful to start the process of mapping lecturers' and administration staff's journey through the institution before and after the merger and how their experiences and perceptions of the institution changed through the merger.

Methodology

A qualitative approach was used in the study. The data presented in this chapter were gathered during four digital storytelling workshops held in 2013 and 2014 with academics and administration staff. Participation at these storytelling workshops was on a voluntary basis: each workshop attracted approximately five participants. Three workshops were held with academic staff members and one with administration members. In total, 20 digital stories were created, 17 by female staff members and 3 by male staff members. The River of Life, a visual brainstorming technique, and the story circle, in which participants shared their stories, two of the key stages of digital storytelling process and where the digital stories are shared and co-created among participants, were used to gather data presented in this chapter. These conversations were recorded and transcribed. The data collected was then analysed deductively by mapping issues arising from the conversations on Archer's social realism model elements. Participants' consent to participate in this study was sought, and ethical clearance for conducting the study was given by the Fundani Centre for Higher Education Development ethics committee. Pseudonyms are used to protect the identity of the participants.

Limitations of the Study

Findings presented in this chapter are opinions from administration and academic staff who may not have a wider perspective of the university; hence, a management perspective is needed to get the full picture.

Findings and Discussion

Findings arising from the data are presented and discussed by mapping out emerging themes along Archer's social realism model elements: structure, culture and agency.

Structure

As indicated earlier, Archer's structural milieu comprises things that exist such as policies, committees as well as more abstract phenomena such as race, gender, social class and knowledge structures in the higher education system (1995, 1996, and 1998). Based on the participants' opinions; vision and mission documents, strategies, policies, institutional transformation office and faculty transformation committees exist at CPUT. However, the impact of these policies, committees or structures is not felt and the picture that emerges is one where most staff are still living in the past and working in silos, as vividly narrated in the following quotes:

Cecilia: And I remember when I was asked to do the presentation that I did in my interview . . . I had a look at CPUT vision and what CPUT stands for. When in actual fact it really, it's just a "nice to have" [. . .] It's not a lived vision, mission. I am sure half of the staff that's here don't even know what the vision and mission say. And so, when it comes back to the work that we do and transformation taking place, people are genuinely doing what they've always done way back then.

Zeta: So while we have all the structures here, at CPUT, we have Fundani, we have Counselling. We have all the faculties but we still operate as separate structures and there isn't a bridge that sort of builds that connection between Fundani and Business, between Fundani and Applied Sciences. And what is interesting that there are structures, there's the Teaching and Learning Committee . . . there are all kinds of committees . . . but somehow you know you can't make an impact on those faculties.

One of the findings showed that staff experienced the support given to them by the institutions to prepare for the merger in 2005 differently. While Liza felt totally unprepared and unsupported, Janice remembers some workshops and meetings that were held around the time of the merger.

Liza: The problem is people who were not prepared for change. There's no workshop that was done, there was no—to me, that's how I will look at it.

Janice: So we had those meetings [institutional forum meetings] once
or twice a semester. . . . I think probably only once, but they
were fantastic meetings because they were meetings discussing
the future and the strategic paths that the Cape Technikon will
take. And I found that very enlightening—the fact that I could be
in a low position as a lecturer and as a senior lecturer being on a
committee like that. But when we became CPUT of course that
fell away and the whole situation changed. The whole situation
changed to become a hierarchical structure, so the structure of
the management of the university became completely hierarchical, because [some] people made the main decisions and they'll
tell the other people what to do and suddenly you were absolutely
nothing.

What many of the participants agreed upon, is a perceived lack of activities
and interventions by the very units and structures that should support ongoing transformation issues:

Lerato: . . . Well, I don't know what that office does but what I know is that
we have meetings after meetings, talking about things that are really
not going to change at our school . . . I've been the Chairperson of
the Transformation Forum [in the faculty] but I really don't see what
its purpose is and what it has achieved.

The lack of action to encourage social cohesion in the University is another
issue raised by participants. They indicated that there was no cohesion, a
sense of belonging as they had felt in their pre-merger institutions. This feeling is captured in the following quotes:

Jane: . . . And so, as I was working for PenTech,[2] it became one big family,
everybody knows everyone . . . [the Rector] that time, he knows you
by the name, whether he sees you outside or wherever. If we have
end of year parties, he dances with all of us, do the Bart Man. It was
like one big family [. . .] [At CPUT] you become a number, yes. You
don't know the people next to you. People don't know each other.
They walk past each other, they don't greet each other. It's just a few
from PenTech's people that are still working in the library that will
at least greet you—the others, they just walk past you. So yes, it's a
feeling of sadness and anger and it's not fun.

Joy: You know we started the Digital Storytelling Project in 2010
and we've researched it and . . . I don't get any support from my
dean, you know I didn't get any from the deputy dean, they're not

interested . . . nothing is done to address social cohesion in our university.

In these comments and more (see the following discussion), there is also a sense that the institution has introduced stronger hierarchical structures, which impact on communication and transparency. With regard to operational issues, administrative staff members, in particular, reported that they felt undermined and disrespected and did not know what was happening in the units unlike before the merger:

Liza: . . . Now, I was once told that there is a power distance between me and senior management. There was a power distance. Maybe that's the reason why when the kitchen was dirty we, all the admin had to be called to be told that we must wash the dishes—maybe that's the power distance that I'm looking at. It's, you know, people there and us there. I don't know.

Jabulo: . . . if you can say that in a space where we are working, . . . you are nothing here. You know, those harsh words, they hit home. As much as you will just [say] okay, that's them and you move on. But being told that you must know that you are nothing here, you are a simple piece of administration, you are constantly reminded you are an administrator here. . . .

Liza: . . . like as a secretary for Fundani [pre-merger], I had a meeting with the director every day. I knew what was happening every day, if it's not an hour, we'll make it 20 minutes. So I knew like right now, when there's a post that is being advertised, I knew about it so when I'm asked about it I will have to answer, but now I will say I don't know what is happening there. There's a post, somebody is phoning, Liza what? I don't know, and that is not a nice thing to say to a person. That you don't know. The workshops that are happening, where are they? I don't know. So that kind of communication of knowing what is happening in all the units.

Furthermore, participants suggested that CPUT had not created spaces for staff members to raise issues without being judged or punished.

Liza: No, if you don't talk, you wouldn't know. But we have never been given the platform. We have never been given the platform to talk about these things, so how are you going to know?

Joy: I've had such a tough three months. I think that it's not worth shouting your mouth out. It's best just to shut up, put your head under the sand and live like that. It's not worth it. I've spoken out . . .—and

> it's been tough. The consequences of speaking out, it's not worth it. It's not worth it.

While there were plans to introduce regular university and faculty assemblies from 2013 (CPUT, 2013), these plans were not implemented as envisaged, as Ben mentions in the following, suggesting the lack of safe spaces for people to air their views:

Ben: . . . I wanted to mentioned the issue of the university assembly . . . because as staff you know, in various departments in faculties have been raising issue of that there are no spaces where people can informally voice their opinions without being judged . . .

Culture

The cultural milieu comprises how and what we think about things. This includes our values, beliefs, attitudes and ideologies (Archer, 1995, 1996, 1998). One of the main themes that emerged from participants comments was the lack of a new shared institutional identity:

Ben: . . . we don't have a shared understanding of what CPUT is about, in terms of our academic identity in particular, you know. Who are we? What do we want to become? You know what are the basic ingredients for us actually to be this great university that Council wants us to become? Are we actually—do we have the right tools? Do we have the right people in the various units at CPUT? Who can really make that visionary I'm not too sure quite frankly.

Jane: . . . 2004, I wrote doomsday. Because that was the last day. That was the day Pentech died because after that it became CPUT. And to [us from] PenTech it seemed like a takeover. I know the CapeTech people feel differently [feel like PenTech took over].

In the absence of a shared identity, as shown in the preceding results, subcultures emerged at CPUT. It became clear that some staff members still identified themselves with their former institutional ways of doing things, as shown in the following quotes:

Cecilia: . . . [V]ery interesting to me is that from 2014 . . . up until last year, there's still the them and us. You still find people referring to no, I come from the CapeTech days and I'm PenTech days and people still refer to them and us. And so even though it's a merged institution people still seem themselves as separate.

Liza: . . . Here at PenTech, when I do a requisition I need to show them, which is PentTech, and us, CapeTech. That's how we saw it because things didn't match. The system, the way we were doing things, and that frustrated us when we have to do things. Like I'll make an example of doing a requisition. If I was doing it in the old CapeTech, I knew the process. It will go from Liza to the Director, from the Director to Finance and Finance to Procurement and people would do that job, follow it up . . . [now I feel] like I'm not being helped because I'm an old CapeTech person . . . When I had to book for the car, somebody would say there's no car. But then if I ask Buyi [ex PenTech staff] to book a car, then Buyi would get the car . . . sorry for mentioning names . . . Yes, that is still happening, even now . . .

Liza's quote also alludes to the fact that operations are affected, as staff members lean into serving the staff from their previous institutions. Participants seemed to be sceptical of whether there will ever be a CPUT identity in the near future:

Jane: No, to me it's not the CapeTech/PenTech thing, although I think for years to come it will still be PenTech—CapeTech, until all the CapeTech and the PenTech people . . .
Liza: Die . . .

There was a strong feeling among participants that management had employed unqualified or incompetent people to positions of power, causing clashes with people who actually had the knowledge and competencies to get the job done. Participants raised the fact that management had a culture of undermining and frustrating competent people at CPUT, which had led to brain drain from the institution:

Judy: But as many other people left, because they felt a disjoint between themselves, their personal values and CPUT and I feel that too. I feel that there is a disjoint and part of that disjoint are things that you're talking about, that people get into positions where they're absolutely not qualified. Then they get into that position and they hold forth and they tell everybody else what to do with no real authority or experience . . . you know people are incompetent but it's kind of—it's really bad for CPUT because you can see what a huge difference a good leader makes. A good leader can really change the course of this river and but they've got to be prepared to step up to the place and they've got to have the skills and the knowledge to do their job. You can't do these complex jobs without the skills and the knowledge to do it . . .

I can tell you the names of half a dozen people at UCT, Stellenbosch Centre for Higher Learning. UWC, Pretoria, all over the place who've left CPUT because they're blocked all the time because they've got these great ideas. They've got vision—they want to do things and they're being blocked.

Additionally, participants lamented that management had a strong culture of brushing negative things under the carpet and showcasing the positive, as indicated in the following conversation:

Ruth: So what is your story?
Joy: I would love to go with the fact that we're not producing any good teachers but that's not good for the university. That's not a good— you know I can't . . .
Judy: That is good for the university. The university must know . . . We must be critical you know. I think there's a strong culture at CPUT of brushing things under the carpet, you know, don't let anybody know about—you know—just say wonderful things and showcase the wonderful things. But this is really important.

Systemic racism, intersected with issues of language, gender and disability, leading to feelings of marginalisation at CPUT, was mentioned in participants' comments:

Judy: But I think it's really interesting because it raises the whole sort of English, Afrikaans thing which isn't—because there is such a big colour, black white, thing. The whole English Afrikaans thing is . . .
Lebo: It is.
Judy: And very much—it does rise to the surface every now and then particularly like in the language committee when something happens.
Joyce: I mean I've got a coloured friend on the Wellington Campus who says, you think you've got a problem being English, try being Coloured. I wasn't Black enough in the past—I wasn't White enough in the apartheid era and now I'm not black enough. They feel marginalized you know . . .
Ben: We don't see anything on people with disabilities. But you say you're transforming. So then we say to that person, what, okay, thank you for bringing . . . but we are not convinced that actually you are committed to bringing people with disability at CPUT. Those are the most marginalized. If you talk about issues of social justice—those are the most marginalized and you have to bring them people. We've got targets that we have failed to meet . . .

Agency

The agentic milieu comprises people. Various logics underpin culture, structure and agency and these can be complementary or contradictory (1995, 1996 and 1998). Participants perceived CPUT as both a place of constraints and opportunities, a place that empowers as well as hinders, as evidenced in the following quotes:

Lerato: But gradually, I realised that CPUT is actually . . . . It's a place of constraints and a place of opportunity and that is the identity, you know I developed of CPUT as a place of two worlds. A constraint because of racism and discrimination and gender you know, gender, race, issues of transformation were constraints but they were also opportunities that CPUT offered me, many opportunities. So now I had to make a personal choice. I was faced with choices now, okay, here are two worlds, you have to choose . . . . I found that CPUT had the resources for me. It had the funding opportunities. It had staff development opportunities on one side, but on the other side I found that there were these issues that I had to grapple with . . .

Ruth: . . . So it's a story of becoming you know, of being recognised and more assured in what I do, success and recognition especially with my promotion to Senior Lecturer and stuff. So for me I don't have many issues. For me it's [CPUT] a place of opportunity . . .

The preceding results show that CPUT is perceived by some staff as a place of constraints as far as racism, race and a lack of transformation are concerned and as a place of opportunity as it affords staff members funding and developments opportunities. Whether or not staff members could take advantage of opportunities or became bogged down by challenges seems to be seen as a personal choice. Participants voiced that some staff members have suppressed the fight for transformation and focused on what empowers them (see Lerato's following comment), while others have undergone personal transformation and taken a stance not to be part of the people who are resisting change (see Joyce's comment).

Lerato: . . . So even now as I stand I am asking myself should I take advantage of the opportunities and ignore issues of transformation that stress me and if I do that—will I be satisfied with where I am with CPUT? Because even though I—you know I take advantage of these opportunities, but I still feel that I'm responsible for you know, for the change that has to occur at CPUT. But now I've decided to just suppress the feelings and move on with what is afforded me . . .

Joyce: I joined CPUT in 2012 and I've always played on my strong English culture and heritage and I've always played on the fact that at least I wasn't one of the oppressors . . . at the beginning of this year, the first challenge I had to overcome as I say there, I hit a brick wall, was the thing about using Afrikaans as an academic language and whether or not it is acceptable or not. And I—coming—looking at my heritage—looking at my background story, being fundamentally anti-Afrikaans—started looking at things from a different perspective and I actually made a fundamental—it was fundamental paradigm shift in my mind. And it wasn't because of politics or language or legacy—it was about the students that sat in my class . . . we have rural Coloured students who cannot speak English and who are Afrikaans and are really good Afrikaans students and I had to make that fundamental shift as a proud English speaking liberal South African to promote Afrikaans. And as I said, it was a huge leap and it was a big splash . . .

Conclusion and Recommendations

This chapter reflects on staff perceptions' on CPUTs merger and in general on the institutional transformation. In the participants' responses, we found pain, nostalgia for old times and feelings of alienation and loneliness. Staff reported different levels of preparation and expressed their continued disbelief that it actually happened. Both respondents from the historical institutions and those employed post-merger indicated that there was and there still is a lack of action to encourage social cohesion and transformation in the university on a multitude of levels (such as not only between staff from the merged institutions but also between merged campuses, admin/academic staff, across language, culture, race and gender). In general, participants stated that the university lacked a shared identity, and hence, subcultures existed and continue to exist, with some of the staff still identifying themselves with their historical institutions. This not only impedes the transformation process in the institution but still causes frustration and discontent, sometimes trauma, and heavily impacts institutional operation, climate and collaboration as well. For some of the participants, it has resulted in leaving the institution altogether. According to Trevor Manuel, a member of parliament and council member (CPUT, 2013, p. 9), "[n]obody wanted the merger", but it happened. An institution formed from products of apartheid, and it still shows. The authors argue in this chapter that the lack of support, care and Ubuntu during the merger process for the affected employees of the institutions still impacts on both pre-merger and post-merger recruited employees—more than 10 years down the line.

Without a concerted effort from all stakeholders at CPUT to work together as an entity, this neglect will continue to hamper the institutional functioning. There is a dire need for CPUT to find ways of ensuring staff members work together towards the achievement of CPUT vision and mission, grounded in CPUT lived values.

Despite the aforementioned issues, the institution has managed to achieve significant successes:

• Out of the universities of technology in the country, CPUT is the only one which has not been placed under administration.
• CPUT is the only university in the country, if not Africa, with a nano satellite.
• CPUT is the only university in the country with three technology stations (Clothing and Textile, Agrifood Technology Station, and TIA Adaptronics Advanced Manufacturing Technology Laboratory).

Based on the findings, the authors recommend that communication is key for all stakeholders at CPUT. This will keep all parties informed of what is happening, achievements and challenges in the institution. Communication should provide the stakeholders with an opportunity to engage with each other in a professional manner and with mutual respect, regardless of rank and file. This may help in bringing a sense belonging.

Only then we will be able to achieve the fundamental mind shift that is needed from all CPUT staff members, a shift that allows us to see beyond race and subcultures, to look at what CPUT as an institution is supposed to achieve while recognising and embracing our complex and messy history and heritage.

Notes

1. STORYCENTER: LISTEN DEEPLY, TELL STORIES. Retrieved from https://www.storycenter.org/.
2. While CPUT is a product of a range of merged institution, the two main institutions that participants refer to are the Peninsula Technikon (PenTech) and the Cape Technikon (CapeTech), the former a formerly coloured institution and the latter a former white institution.

References

Archer, M. S. (1995). *Realist social theory: The morphogenetic approach*. Cambridge: Cambridge University Press.
Archer, M. S. (1996). *Culture and agency: The place of culture in social theory*. Cambridge: Cambridge University Press.
Archer, M. S. (1998). Social theory and the analysis of society. In T. May & M. Williams (Eds.), *Knowing the social world*. Buckingham: Open University Press.

Bozalek, V. G. (2011). Acknowledging privilege through encounters with difference: Participatory Learning and Action techniques for decolonising methodologies in Southern contexts. *International Journal of Social Research Methodology, 14*(6), 469–484.

Bozalek, V. G., & Biersteker, L. (2010). Exploring power and privilege using participatory learning and action techniques. *Social Work Education, 29*(5), 551–572. https://doi.org/10.1080/02615470903193785

Cape Peninsula University of Technology. (2013, July 27). Inaugural University Assembly, Bellville Campus.

Hay, D., & Fourie, M. (2002). Preparing the way for mergers in South African higher and further education institutions: An investigation into staff perceptions. *Higher Education, 44*, 115–131.

Lambert, J. (2009). Where it all started: The center for digital storytelling in California. In J. Hartley & K. McWilliam (Eds.), *Story circle: Digital storytelling around the world* (pp. 79–90). Chichester: Wiley-Blackwell.

Lambert, J. (2010). *Digital storytelling: Cookbook.* Center for Digital Storytelling. Retrieved from https://wrd.as.uky.edu/sites/default/files/cookbook.pdf

Seepe, S. (2010, November 28). South Africa: Reflections on a major merger. *University World News.* South Africa, Issue No. 67.

Theme 6

What additional policies, practices and initiatives would be beneficial in further advancing the transformation of higher education at Cape Peninsula University of Technology and broadly at institutions of higher education throughout South Africa?

7 Towards Critical Citizenship Education—A Case Study in an Architectural Technology and Interior Design Extended Curriculum Course

Alex Noble and Daniela Gachago

Introduction

Since the end of apartheid, South African higher education has undergone major transformations, concerned both with widening access and with the kinds of students we would like to produce. The 2008 Report of the Ministerial Committee on Transformation and Social Cohesion and the Elimination of Discrimination in Public Higher Education Institutions, for example, called for the production of "enlightened, responsible and constructively critical citizens" (Soudien et al., 2008, p. 90). More recently, and in the context of debates about the decolonisation of the curriculum, questions about what should be taught, how, where and who should be teaching have become paramount. Critical citizenship, the focus of this chapter, nevertheless remains at the core of the transformation agenda.

The architectural curriculum has long been challenged for its lack of engagement with social justice. Saidi (2005, p. 206) argued that issues such as housing and transformation of the architectural profession do not receive adequate attention: "The architecture profession has been viewed to serve the interests of an elite population. The education process of architects has been designed to replicate this relationship". Ten years later, Osman (2015) argued, "Architecture is a profession that may offer spatial, technical and social expertise to serve large segments of the population. Yet it remains relatively disengaged, isolated, untransformed and elitist".

These criticisms are not limited to South Africa. The 2014 Union of International Architects Student Charter argued that "the value and relevance of architectural education is becoming increasingly scrutinized in light of pressing socio-economic conditions, which demand OTHER ways of engagement and transformation in the way we think about and practice architecture" (p. 4).

In order for the architectural profession to change, we feel it impera-tive that teaching practices and curriculum foci must change. The high school curriculum does not adequately address enduring post-apartheid inequality, lending additional urgency to the need for architecture schools to develop a more critical curriculum. Yet university teaching still falls short of this goal for many reasons: not only curriculum requirements, workload, time constraints, the need to work towards industry expecta-tions and accreditation—but also fear of tackling sensitive issues such as race and privilege in diverse classrooms. This chapter reflects on an attempt to respond to the call for critical citizenship through a series of experiential and experimental projects implemented with Extended Cur-riculum Programme (ECP) Architectural Technology and Interior Design students in the first semester of the 2017 academic year.

Storytelling for Critical Citizenship Within the Context of the Built Environment

In a time of global anxiety about migration and its impacts, the notion of citi-zenship is highly contested. What does it mean to be a citizen? What rights and duties come with citizenship? What does it mean to be a critical citizen working within the built environment? If we accept that ethno-nationalistic forms of identity need to be challenged (Johnson & Morris, 2010), what understanding of citizenship should frame our teaching? What shared values can we promote or negotiate? What would allow us to move away from mod-els based on normative frameworks that reproduce hegemonic discourses and set up binaries (Bozalek & Carolissen, 2012) towards a model that allows us to challenge fixed notions of identity and embrace fluidity and social cohe-sion? What would it mean to, as Dejaeghere (2009, p. 231) suggests, "allow teachers and students to bring their lived experiences and constructions of citizenship to engage with issues facing citizens in all strata of our societies"? This chapter is an attempt to answer some of these questions we have been struggling with in our teaching practice.

Lister (1997, p. 3) defines citizenship simply as "the relationship between individuals and the state and between individual citizens within [the] com-munity". In South Africa, the legacy of apartheid still complicates relation-ships between people from different racial and cultural backgrounds. Zinn and Rodgers (2013, p. 77) argue that

> [i]f relationships have been fraught with and characterised by systemic injustice, as has been the case in South Africa, then this has necessarily damaged and distorted conceptions of citizenship. The pursuit of social justice becomes an imperative and driver, as citizens strive both to be

fully recognized and to have their right to belong fully to that society restored.

This is even more important for the so-called "born-free" generation, raised on a "rainbow discourse" (Gachago & Ngoasheng, 2016), which in general discouraged an engagement with race, inequality and the legacies of apartheid in the name of nation building. Critical citizenship education, in our view, then needs to create spaces within which students can question their own notions of identity, and the identities of those they consider "other," in order to allow a new engagement across difference. In the context of the built environment, this translates into developing a recognition and critical understanding of one's own position within and towards the built environment and within the spatial legacies of colonialism and apartheid.

This kind of teaching is done both in the classroom and in communities to expose students "to other cultures and disciplines through travel and local community engagement" as "culture is an integral to the creation of good architecture" (UIA, 2014, pp. 10–13). We strongly believe that if architecture in South Africa is to become more responsive, we need to take The International Union of Architects (UIA) Student Charter's recommendations for "architecture as a catalyst for socio-economic development" (2014, p. 12) seriously. The charter argues that architectural education and practice must become more sensitive of, and responsive toward, social issues by drawing from fields such as sociology and history in order for students "to have an ethical responsibility to act with empathy and be mindful of the social context" (p. 13).

As an overarching theoretical framework, we use *storytelling* as a tool towards critical citizenship that is culturally and socially sensitive, empathetic and mindful of social context. Storytelling is a sociocultural practice, with inherent power relations between storyteller and listener, that foregrounds individual agency, voices, emotions and creativity (Stein, 2008). It is also a meaning-making practice in which storyteller and audience co-construct stories. We believe student voices, experiences and narratives should be central within a critical, decolonized curriculum, so this project from which data for this chapter are derived placed a strong emphasis on personal storytelling. On their field trips, students listened to a wide range of personal stories that linked the past to the present, urban development to rural settlement and busy city life to a quiet rural life. But students were also encouraged to tell their own stories in various ways—orally, in writing and multimodally as digital stories (Reed & Hill, 2012). By sharing these stories, we hoped that students could begin not only to see themselves in new ways but also to gain an understanding of how their identities are bound up with others around them.

Context of the Study From Which Data Presented in This Chapter Were Drawn

The ECP in the Department of Architectural Technology and Interior Design aims to increase access into the disciplines for students who have recognized potential but whose secondary schooling did not prepare them sufficiently for university. ECP students extend their first year of study across two years, undergoing a series of additional classes and experiences to bring them up to speed with the mainstream programme.

The course is taught through project-based learning, linking all subjects to a main design project. This helps students understand the integration of design across all subjects, allowing for a scaffolding of knowledge embedded in the design projects while encouraging the development of students' own sense of agency. An important component of the programme is to expose students to differences in the built environment and divisions in South African society.

Since 2015, the programme has included field trips to the District Six Museum, Homecoming Centre and a site near the university campus and to the Moravian village of Genadendal. These sites were chosen for their historical relevance: Genadendal for its historical rural development by the Moravian Church and its relation to local Khoisan inhabitants and District Six for its more recent history of forced removals as well as its entanglement with Cape Peninsula University of Technology (CPUT), which was built on the site of these removals. As both these sites engage primarily, although not exclusively, with "Coloured"[1] history, we also included a field trip to Robben Island, where Nelson Mandela and many other political activists were imprisoned during apartheid. The following section describes these activities and projects in more detail.

The ECP Architectural Technology and Interior Design Critical Citizenship Curriculum

In order to facilitate students' engagement with self, other and the built environment, we redesigned the ECP curriculum to include projects in which students reflect on how their own identity, their relationship with their peers and the built environment are impacted by past and present.

Project 1: Linking Self, Other and the Built Environment— The Identity Project

This is a collaborative "vertical project" where students from ECP up to Baccalaureus Technologiae (BTech) explore issues of identity relating to self and other. Working in groups, students come up with a group identity and, relating abstract ideas to form, build an individual concept cardboard model of "self," which links with their group-identity collective model. After the collaborative project, each ECP student does a second project on identity, this time relating his or her personal identity to buildings, spaces and furniture. Students explore their own personal identity in relation to their culture, their traditions, their peers and their personal ideas of themselves, investigating who they feel they are while researching buildings and spaces and the designers whose work demonstrates these ideas while at the same time grappling with concepts of scale, proportion and learning to draft and build scale models.

Project 2: Linking Past and Present, Self and Society— District Six, Robben Island and the Privilege Walk

The second project begins with an historical lecture on the development of Cape Town, covering the arrival of Dutch settlers in the 1600s and the encounter with the Khoisan, occupation by the English, the apartheid era, the Group Areas Act and other apartheid laws which affected the city's landscape socially and spatially over the past 400 years. District Six becomes the focus of this project: a bulldozed former urban settlement in the heart of the city identified within the notion of "de-settlement." During a two-day workshop with the District Six Museum and Homecoming Centre students learn more about South African history and, in particular, about the forced removals of the late 1960s. They reflect on the complexity of apartheid's legacies and how these still play out today, as seen in our institution's silence around its own implications in the D6 history. Students work with former residents who share stories and memories, guide them around the museum and take them out to former landmark roads and sites of buildings. From these activities, the students develop short personal narratives about their own experiences and the stories told by the former residents, collecting imagery and taking notes to be later developed into a digital story. The students also visit Robben Island to broaden their historical knowledge of apartheid.

Students also participate in an activity called the Privilege Walk. The Privilege Walk, in its original format, is a series of statements around living conditions and lived experience developed to help students recognize their own, often invisible, privilege (McIntosh, 1992). Framed by critical pedagogy (Freire, 1970) and with a focus on the intersectionality of privilege, this activity forces students to acknowledge their position in a privilege grid that poignantly represents the current state of our society. Statements focus not only on race but also on how race, gender, class, sexuality, age, religion, able-bodiedness, safety and so on intersect. This allows students to see privilege as more than financial advantage and more than just white privilege and

Figure 7.1 Workshop with students at the District Six Homecoming Center

forces them to think about their own social positioning in relation to their peers within the larger South African society. Students reflect again on these experiences in the form of short reflective narratives.

Project 3: Linking the Urban and the Rural—A Visit to Genadendal

The third project consists of a four-day field trip to the Moravian missionary settlement Genadendal, set up by Moravian missionaries in the mid-1700s alongside an existing Khoisan settlement. Genadendal is unique in South Africa: It is inhabited by a mixed-race community that can trace lineages back to Khoisan, Indonesian and German heritage; and as it doesn't sit as an annex next to a previously classified "White" settlement. The students experience the "genius loci"[2] of a formal efarly settlement, at the same time learning the tactile skills of the profession by measuring up street thresholds and doing observational drawings of the main town square or "werf" and surroundings. They also meet local historians who take the students around the town and into the museums, telling stories about historical development and settlement over the past 300 years.

Figure 7.2 Students outside the Moravian church in Genadendal

Methodology

This study from which data was taken for this paper follows a qualitative research design. The 28 participants are drawn from the 2017 ECP Architectural Technology and Interior Design student cohort (of 30 in total). Of the 28 students, the majority are Coloured, and about a third are African; there is a balanced male-to-female ratio (see Table 7.1).

The data collection instruments consisted of two surveys, conducted before and after the three projects, which probed for students' perceptions of self and other and their understanding and relationship to South African history. The post-survey also included questions on critical thinking and how students linked the interventions to their professional identity as designers. Twenty-eight (28) students completed survey 1, and 18 students completed survey 2 (14 students completed both surveys). Students were also asked to write reflective narratives after their visit to the District Six Museum and Homecoming Centre and the Privilege Walk exercise.

Table 7.1 Student demographics

Race	Number	Percentage
African (A)	9	32
Coloured (C)	16	57
Indian (I)	2	7
White (W)	1	4
Gender		
Female (F)	15	50
Male (M)	15	50

Open-ended questions in the surveys and the narratives were analysed thematically by the two authors of this chapter, first individually and then collaboratively. Examples of survey comments and anonymised extracts from student narratives are included in the findings. As identity is such an important factor in this study, we identify students by race and gender where possible (W = White, C = Coloured, A = African, F = Female, M = Male). Ethical clearance was sought through institutional channels, and students gave informed consent.

Findings

Four main themes which emerged from the data analysis were localised socio-historical and political awareness, shifts in students' perceptions of self and other, the power of affect and the integration of personal and professional identity.

Localised Socio-Historical and Political Awareness of Apartheid's Spatial Legacies

A strong theme emerging from the data was the students' identification with and understanding of history as localised and often racialised: students identified with the history that was *close* to them. The following survey comments, for example, revealed personal and intergenerational entanglement with the history of District Six:

> My grandmother worked in District Six and the history of District Six affected my grandmother and (her) family (C/F).

> My family was moved from District 6 to Heideveld and Manenberg (C/M).

My grandparents and father grew up there and the history still runs in the family (C/F).

African students and those who didn't grow up in Cape Town seemed to be far less connected to District Six, although some still related to a collective narrative of forced removals, struggle and hardship beyond geographical boundaries:

I do not know what happened to District 6 (survey 1).

. . . at some point . . . I do (relate) because I might not know back then— but probably my ancestors were forcefully removed from their homes (survey 2) (A/M).

I do (identify) because as a child that grew up in the Eastern Cape, what happened in District Six happened also in (the) Eastern Cape so I can say I know the pain and suffering (A/F).

On the whole, African students related more than the other students to Robben Island:

I strongly identify also in terms of how black people were treated (A/F).

Some students identified with neither history:

It means nothing to me (A/M, survey 1).

I strongly don't identify (A/F, survey 1).

Students who identified themselves as "born frees" struggled to see the continued impact of apartheid on their lives, as the following student explains: "I'm a born free, but as much as I am born free, what happened in the past struggle is the reason why I'm born free, I want to define my own new path" (A/M, survey 1).

Shifts in Students' Perceptions of Self and Other

Another strong theme was the importance of learning about self and other. Students talked, for example, about how seeing their peers move forward and backward during the Privilege Walk made them look beyond their usual assumptions:

Seeing some of my peers more behind or in front of me made me feel a bit uncomfortable because I have never really expected their lives to be perceived in that way. (C/M).

> You can't judge a book by its cover . . . it showed me that my assumptions were completely off. (C/F).

Students also talked about how learning about others increased a sense of connection and belonging:

> I learnt new things about myself and I think it's brought the ECP class closer. (C/M).

> I started to feel connected to them in a sense that we shared the same struggle. It also made me feel that I'm not alone. (C/M).

Many of the students mentioned that they usually don't think about privilege and its impact on their lives:

> It was shocking to see that as a coloured male how privileged I am. (C/M).

> I have never thought about privileges until that very moment. (C/F).

They also started seeing privilege as intersectional; that beyond money or race, issues like gender and sexuality also matter:

> It made me realise that money is not the only privilege. (C/F).

> People are still judged heavily on race and gender. (C/M).

> The purpose of the Privilege Walk is to learn about how people benefit or are treated by systems in our society because of our race, gender or sexuality. (C/M).

They also reflected on the importance of knowing where they stand in society. For some this curiosity was the motivation to do the walk:

> I was even more eager to know where I stood in society. (C/M).

> It is important to know who you are and where you stand in the economy. (A/F).

> Understanding and acknowledging privilege is key to understanding why and how we react and perceive our surroundings. (C/M).

The experience seemed to have had a lasting impact on some students, as this comment shows: "It taught me a lot cause I feel like . . . my mindset changed and lately I have been seeing things differently" (A/M).

There is also evidence of an emerging understanding of how the legacy of apartheid still impacts on students' lived experiences and opportunities to succeed, challenging dominant discourses around meritocracy:

> I found out that because of events of the past and as well of the present, many of [my peers] have to put much more effort to do the things they need to get done. (C/M).

> Some will have to put in much more effort than others to achieve the same results because of the lack of privileges to assist them. (C/F).

> The injustice of the past is still ever present in today's society, the Privilege Walk is a brilliant tool and creates . . . setting in which we as a people can have these awkward conversations where we can begin to rebuild a greater tomorrow. (C/M).

The Power of Affect

These kinds of teaching interventions inevitably brought up a range of emotions. Many students reflected, for example, on nervousness, discomfort and even anxiety experienced during the Privilege Walk:

> [A]s the uncomfortable yet real questions were being said. (C/F).

> [D]eep thoughts and emotions about my life arose. (C/F).

> I was scared that if the lecturer asked me [what I felt], I was going to cry, but she didn't and I was relieved. (A/F).

> I entered the Privilege Walk being anxious, nervous and unsure. (I/F).

The Privilege Walk, in particular, was resisted by some of the students. A handful left the room before the walk started, and a few left midway. In their reflections, students mentioned how some of the questions triggered brought up past traumas:

> It affected some of us more than others, because it dug out buried thoughts, forgotten thoughts, thoughts that we didn't ever want to bring up again because those thoughts left scars on our hearts (C/F).

> I felt so isolated . . . I have always been one to look past all the bad memories but now I was standing face to face with it I did not want to walk away from it (once again) but I was overwhelmed. Escaping has always been my defense mechanism (C/F).

Integration of Personal and Professional Identity

While some students struggled to see the relevance of the interventions in terms of their disciplines, in other cases an understanding of the entanglement of personal and professional identity emerged (all taken from survey 2):

> I discovered that we as humans put up fronts and seem a certain way yet we learn to ignore things that eat us up inside, preventing us to move forward and find ourselves. What I understand about why we did this walk was because in architecture we have to know ourselves to know what our architectural style would be and what messages and emotion we will put into our buildings . . . . for us to become great we need to know ourselves but do it on our own terms [in our] own way. (C/M).

> I have discovered more about me in terms of my own creative style as well as me as an individual. (C/M).

> Because ever since I had class learning about my identity, [my] perspective has changed a lot. The plan[ned] project learning to identify sub-urban and rural area[s] has challenged my mind and improved my knowledge. Also the history from both places gave me a great history of my country, knowing where we come from and where we are now. (A/M).

In some students' responses, we also found a sensitivity towards the particular conditions, such as working with limited resources, that they will encounter in their practice, and a growing passion for social justice:

> I have a greater understanding of myself now . . . speaking about space, meeting the [people's] needs. Working with limited resources, introducing a public outlook on a town/space etc. (C/F).

> I have been on a path of discovery this past few years but our assignments really made me focus on my identity. It links up with architecture because it shows us that we have a great task of uniting us as a people through design. I'd like to be a cautious designer. Not just [to] design pretty buildings, but design buildings that will bring about a change in lives and these projects helped me make that decision. (C/M).

> The PW really sensitised me to some of the many issues we are facing as a country and the social responsibility to change things. (C/M).

> It is in our own hands to determine whether we continue the cycle or work harder to break it and close the gap. (C/F).

It made me want to change the future for myself and my children in future, in fact I don't want to change only for myself but for other children in my country who are in the same shoes as me. (A/F).

Discussion and Conclusion

We have reflected on a range of interventions introduced to allow students' to engage with self and other and with the built environment as first steps towards a critical citizenship education. We were particularly interested in the extent to which these interventions allowed a shift in our students' sense of self, other and community—and, ultimately, in their perception of their place and role in the architectural discipline. The idea of starting the programme with an identity project was to help students better understand themselves and the reasons for which they had chosen these disciplines. By using historically rich focus areas of study, the students were also able to learn basic disciplinary skills in addition to listening and sharing stories about South Africa's past and present.

Findings showed that students' knowledge of the legacy of apartheid is limited and fragmented, linked to a particular context of upbringing—confirming the continued social segregation of South African society based on race, language and culture. We saw a sense of detachment from history in general, an impatience and desire to "move on." We argue that this is common among this generation of students who have grown up in post-apartheid South Africa, where engagement on issues of race, gender and age was not necessarily encouraged and students were fed on a "rainbow nation discourse" (Ngoasheng & Gachago, 2017). However, we also found a growing understanding of the interrelatedness of past and present, the importance of personal storytelling in challenging assumptions and beliefs students carried about each other and an understanding of identity and privilege as something that carries multiple layers and is complex, intersectional and fluid (Crenshaw, 1989).

We must be aware of the complexities of engaging in these difficult conversations, the many emotions that issues such as race and privilege evoke in students, the possibility of triggering trauma and the importance of considering the ethical implications of such interventions.

Most encouragingly, we saw students start linking their personal identity to a professional identity, demonstrating a budding sense of responsibility for each other and the future of South Africa as socially conscious, or "cautious" designers and architects, as one of the students put it.

The commitment to conscientising students is neither simple nor quick. It needs a careful balancing of practical, experiential, theoretical skills and interdisciplinary knowledge to grow well-rounded professionals and future leaders. What we have not done in this project, but could be an extension of this research, is include students in curriculum co-design, another call by the student movements.

Notes

1. *Coloured* is a term formalised under apartheid in South Africa to refer to those South Africans loosely bound together for historical reasons rather than by common ethnic identity (Erasmus & Pieterse, 1999). In the Western Cape, where they are referred to as "Cape Coloureds", their ancestry may include European colonisers, indigenous Khoisan, Xhosa people and slaves imported from the Dutch East Indies.
2. 'Genius of Space'/'Genius Loci' is the prevailing character or atmosphere of place. The concept is found in *Genius Loci: Towards a Phenomenology of Architecture* (Christian Norberg-Schulz, 1979).

References

Bozalek, V. G., & Carolissen, R. (2012). The potential of critical feminist citizenship frameworks for citizenship and social justice in higher education University of Western Cape. *Perspectives in Education*, *30*(4), 9–18.

Crenshaw, K. (1989). Demarginalizing the intersection of race and sex: A black feminist critique of antidiscrimination doctrine, feminist theory and antiracist politics. *University of Chicago Legal Forum*, *140*, 139–167.

Dejaeghere, J. G. (2009). Critical citizenship education for multicultural societies. *Revista Interamericana de Eduacion Para La Democracia*, *2*(2), 223–246.

Erasmus, Z., & Pieterse, E. (1999). Conceptualising coloured identities in the Western Cape province of South Africa. In M. Palmberg (Ed.), *National identity and democracy in Africa* (pp. 167–187). Cape Town: Human Sciences Research Council.

Freire, P. (1970). *Pedagogy of the oppressed.* 30th Anniversary Edition. New York: The Continuum International Publishing Group Inc.

Gachago, D., & Ngoasheng, A. (2016, October 19). South Africa's rainbow nation is a myth that students need to unlearn. *The Conversation*. Retrieved from https://theconversation.com/south-africas-rainbow-nation-is-a-myth-that-students-need-to-unlearn-66872

Johnson, L., & Morris, P. (2010). Towards a framework for critical citizenship education. *The Curriculum Journal*, *21*(1), 77–96. http://doi.org/10.1080/09585170903560444

Lister, R. (1997). *Citizenship: Feminist perspectives.* New York: New York University Press.

McIntosh, P. (1992). White privilege: Unpacking the invisible knapsack. In A. M. Filor (Ed.), *Multiculturalism* (pp. 30–36). New York: New York State Council of Educational Associations. Retrieved from http://files.eric.ed.gov/fulltext/ED355141.pdf#page=43

Ngoasheng, A., & Gachago, D. (2017). Dreaming up a new grid: Two lecturers' reflections on challenging traditional notions of identity and privilege in a South African classroom. *Education as Change*, *21*(2), 187–207.

Norberg-Schulz, C. (1979). *Genius Loci: Towards a phenomenology of Architecture*. ebook. Retrieved from https://www.scribd.com/doc/91074765/Genius-Loci-Towards-a-Phenomenology-of-Architecture-Christian-Norberg-Schulz-1979-eBook

Osman, A. (2015). What architects must learn from South African student protests. *The Conversation*. Retrieved from https://theconversation.com/what-architects-must-learn-from-south-african-student-protests-50678

Reed, A., & Hill, A. (2012). "Don't keep it to yourself!": Digital storytelling with South African youth. *International Journal for Media, Technology and Lifelong Learning*, *8*(2). Retrieved from http://seminar.net/index.php/component/content/article/75-current-issue/146-dont-keep-it-to-yourself-digital-storytelling-with-south-african-youth

Saidi, F. E. (2005). *Developing a curriculum model for architectural education in a culturally changing South Africa* (Unpublished doctoral thesis). University of Pretoria, Pretoria.

Soudien, C., Michaels, W., Mthembi-Mahanyele, S., Nkomo, M., Nyanda, G., Nyoka, N., . . . Villa-Vicencio, C. (2008). *Report of the ministerial committee on transformation and social cohesion and the elimination of discrimination in public higher education institutions*. Pretoria: Department of Education.

Stein, P. (2008). *Multimodal pedagogies in diverse classrooms: Representation, rights and resources*. London and New York: Routledge.

UIA. (2014, August 3–7). *The UIA Durban student charter on architecture*. XXV World Congress of Architecture, Durban. Retrieved from http://uj-unit2.co.za/wp-content/uploads/2015/02/UIA-2014-Durban-Student-Charter-1.pdf

Zinn, D., & Rodgers, C. (2013). A humanising pedagogy: Getting beneath the rhetoric. *Perspectives in Education*, *30*(4), 76–87. Retrieved from www.ajol.info/index.php/pie/article/view/86258%5Cnhttp://reference.sabinet.co.za/webx/access/electronic_journals/persed/persed_v30_n4_a9.pdf

8 Exploring Decolonization in South African Higher Education

Potential for Change

Siya Sabata and Monwabisi K. Ralarala

Introduction

This chapter details a theoretical approach developed for a curriculum transformation project driven from the Centre for Higher Education and Development (CHED) at a University of Technology (UoT). The project seeks to respond towards calls for decolonization of South African higher education (HE) following the unprecedented student protests which engulfed South African higher education in the 2015, 2016 and 2017 academic years, respectively. Central to the student protests was unequivocal call for free and decolonized HE (Badat, 2016; Ndlovu-Gatsheni, 2018). The call itself echoed an old critique of the colonial academy from Black/African scholars as far back as the early 1960s, and these include people such as W. E. B. Du Bois, Frantz Fanon, Aime Cesaire, Leopold Senghor, Ngugi wa Thiongo, Archie Mafeje, Thandika Mkhandawire, Molefi Asante, Bernard Magubane and Paulin, J. Hountondji, to name but a few.

In this project, we intend to use our knowledge and expertise in collaboration with actors interested in the project of decoloniality[1] in South Africa, in the broader African continent and globally (in particular, the global South) to create transformative learning opportunities and facilitate epistemic justice[2] for all.

We therefore seek to develop a "learning culture"[3] (James, 2014) that cultivate agency[4] for decolonization. This is an attempt to engage with the social relations of power that facilitate unequal distribution (Bernstein, 2000) of knowledge and power in the "post" colonial-cum-apartheid South African university. We see this as a counterhegemonic curriculum[5] project, which views curriculum development as an ongoing process that requires "constant critique of domination, of institutions and of repressive forms of authority" (Manen, 1977, p. 227). We want to cultivate agency (Archer, 2016) to enhance our transformative praxis in our quest for epistemic justice (Fricker,

2013) for our students. This practice-based approach (praxis) hopes to bring together students, tutors, academics, academic leaders and managers in a project which its main objective is to interrogate historical structured "post"-colonial-cum-apartheid higher education so that changes can be effected. This project is led by Black academics, working in solidarity with all those concerned with continuing educational inequalities and epistemic violence that characterize the "post"-colonial university. We strongly believe in the significance of agents' participation in determining their needs and aspirations in struggles towards their own emancipation (Bhaskar, 1986). But we are equally aware that for this to succeed we would need collective efforts through solidarity. Bhaskar captures this nicely as he says,

> Insofar as emancipation depends upon the transformation of structures, and such structures are general (extensive), a self-emancipatory politics, oriented to that transformation of unwanted and unnecessary sources of determination, will of course need to be a mass (extensive) one. But such a politics need not be necessary for the transformation of particular or local constraints or for constraints stemming from the subjective (psychological) conditions, (poiesological) forms or (praxiological) effects as distinct from the objective (socio-structural) conditions of action.
>
> (1986, p. 176)

This chapter starts off by explaining critical realism as a meta-theoretical framework which guided the development of this curriculum transformation project.

Meta-Theory

In developing a theoretical approach for curriculum transformation, in this case we were guided by critical realism (Bhaskar, 1978; Archer, 1979, 2003) as the meta-theoretical framework. Central to Bhaskar's critical realism (CR) is his notion of depth ontology that is predicated on his view around the existence of the "real" world of unobservable structures that condition our lives even if we know or we do not about them. This is called intransitive[6] world and is stratified. In this stratification, we have structures, powers and mechanisms (the real), the events which they generate (the actual) and the subset of events that are actually (the empirical) experienced. Using CR for this project, we took into cognizance the fact that we cannot begin to talk about a transformation of HE without engaging with the "real" structure, that is, mechanisms and powers (real-intransitive world) that generate events that affect experiences of the people in the present. Our approach was therefore influenced by this clear understanding of the presence of this past on what people are able to do, see and be (human agency) in the present (Bhaskar, 1978; Donati, 2016). We therefore considered the effects of colonialism and apartheid to those who were deemed nonhuman and in need of guidance from their superior colonial masters. While critical realism remains underdeveloped to advance struggles of those who continue to suffer under the bondage of coloniality, its philosophical under-laboring holds potential for radical theoretical advancements in this context. Furthermore, our theoretical leanings and trust toward CR were bolstered by reading Archer's (1979) *Social Origins of Education System*, which subsequently became the origins of her Morphogenetic Approach (MA). In this seminal work, Archer (ibid) developed powerful sociological grounds to account for the dynamics of change (or lack of) in institutions and organizations constituted through distinctive geohistorical processes. Through this work, we now have a sociological approach that allows us to explain what "really" (socio-historical material) had happened rather than some abstract/ ideal world presented through theories trying to homogenize experiences and present universal propositions. She was therefore critical of both Basil Bernstein's and Pierre Bourdieu's theoretical projects as she viewed them as ahistorical or generic and thereby not able to account for peculiarities in differently structured educational systems. Archer's work is famously known for her insistence on the analytic separation between structure/culture and agency.

This separation is premised on her understanding that structure, culture and agency are "temporally distinguishable" (1995, p. 66); in this sense, it is possible to determine what happened when while also possible to trace changes over time. This allows for the account of activities of people in a particular geohistorical context and time; hence, the process is known as "the historicity of emergence."

This theorization vindicates work of earlier Black/African scholars like W. E. B Du Bois and Frantz Fanon, whose works have long been calling for "the historicity of emergence" to account for the emergence of racialized socio-historical material in the postcolonial societies. In their work, racism has been viewed as socio-structural rather than biological natural category. In this way, a racist society could be traced from the inception of modernity around colonialism and imperialism. Bonilla-Silva describes a racialized social system as a society in which "economic, social, political and ideological levels are partially structured by placement of actors on racial categories or races" (1997, p. 496). Mills (2017, p. 5), drawing from this heritage delineates between structure (institutions, practices and social systems, policies) and culture/ideational (a complex set of ideas, beliefs and values) in exactly the same way in which Archer, draws these distinctions. This theoretical framework brought to the fore distinctive social ontology to understand effects of colonialism (neo/post) and became the basis of reimagining new possibilities for those working within Critical

Race Theory and its other variants. While not explored or developed in criti-cal realism, as Hartwig (2016) rightly observed, it is our view that this work is grounded in a realist ontology and therefore sufficient to account complexities in our context. South Africa bears scars of "overtly racist regime" called apart-heid, similar to the US South under Jim Crow and Nazi Germany (Fredrickson, 2002, cited from Mills, 2015). According to Fredrickson (ibid), such societies were characterized with official racist ideology, racial purity as an ideal, man-datory de jury segregation, prohibition on the political activity (such as vot-ing, holding public office) of the oppressed and the deliberate impoverishment of the subordinated race(s). This created systemic structuring advantaging of Whites over Black people and continues to do so even after the demise of the colonial juridical system. Using Bhaskar's threefold reality, we then postulate that in the "real-intransitive world" we have a socio-historical structured mate-rial, which Mills (1997) calls "White supremacy." This speaks to a system of taken-for-granted beliefs and practices of actors in society that perpetuate the dominant position of White people. He describes White supremacy as follows:

> [White supremacy] . . . is the unnamed political system that has made the modern world what it is today . . . the most important political system of recent global history—the system of domination by which white people have historical ruled over and, in certain important ways, continue to rule over nonwhite people—is not seen as a political system at all. It is just taken for granted; it is the background against which other systems, which are to see as political, are highlighted.
>
> (Mills, 1997, p. 1–2)

This is actualized (or remain dormant when not actualized) as events in vari-ous institutions and organization even though mediated differently in various parts of the world and institutions. The empirical reality manifests and is observed as experiences in our day-to-day interactions in various parts of the world.

Manifestation of White Supremacy in South African HE—Empirical Observations

Higher education continues to perpetuate racial education inequalities with student throughput and completion rates remaining racialized. Black students (in particular, African and Coloured) continue to perform at the worst end of the spectrum (CHE, 2012, and 2013). Efforts towards restructuring of HE landscape through university mergers and the creation of new taxonomy of HE institutional types also failed to dismantle the colonial-cum-apartheid "racialized" university structure. As Cooper (2015) observed, despite restruc-turing through mergers the system continues to reproduce social inequalities based on what he calls "race-class" position. It has been noted that "conservative institutional policies and cultures" remain a significant constraint towards demographic change in the academic profiles of South African academics (Mamdani, 2004). Generally, the professoriate remains significantly White in South African universities despite efforts and programmes geared to grow the number of Black academics (CHE, 2016).

Responding to the Crisis

There have been various (even though poorly theorized) pedagogic interventions and support for students in response to this crisis (Teaching Development Grants, University Capacity Development Grant, Extended Curriculum Programmes and other mis-framed projects). However, this is merely a tinkering exercise as the colonial structure (intransitive reality) remains unidentified or at worse ignored. This is not to say that people are not talking about curriculum development initiatives, even though as such it is merely idealism. We have witnessed the establishment of the National Qualification Frameworks; South African Qualification Framework leading Outcomes Based Education; Institutional Audits and Programme Accreditation, Higher Education Qualification Sub-Framework, 2013; and other mechanisms but nothing at all coming closer to the engagement with the colonial structure. In our context as UoT, this tinkering (atheoretical and ahistorical) exercise creates institutional schizophrenia and stress to those expected fill-in "mounds of paper of a bureaucratic kind" to quote (Kraak & Mahomed, 2001).

This could be described as "curriculum development without curriculum theory/or expertise" or what Giroux (2010) calls "bare pedagogy." However, there are some efforts toward curriculum engagement as acknowledged in the following.

Knowledge Without Knowers

It is important to acknowledge various studies theorizing curriculum in South African HE. These studies have illuminated interesting debates about the importance of disciplinary knowledge in curriculum (school curricula and, to a lesser extent, in HE). Drawing from the work of a British sociologist Basil Bernstein, scholars such as Muller (2008), Allais (2003), and Kotta (2008), to name but few, have engaged with the underlying structuring principles of knowledge. Similarly, Shay (2016), Luckett (2009), Winberg (2012) and others have used Karl Maton's Legitimation Code Theory (LCT; Maton, 2005, 2014) in their efforts to interrogate curriculum and pedagogy. While interrogation of knowledge structures and the importance of disciplinary knowledge in curriculum is a significant move, we believe this should not be exclusive from the activities of people in the past (Archer, 1979). It is our view that these studies downplay the role of power relations or the relational network structure of South African HE. Following Maton (2005, 2014), we argue that debates about knowledge/curriculum should always entail engagement with both knowledge and knowers.

Black Nationalism and the Counterhegemonic Curriculum Transformation Project

In South Africa, voices of Black people have long been marginalized in curriculum debates, thanks to many years of exclusionary colonial-cum-apartheid HE system (Fataar, 2006; Muller, 2009). During the apartheid era, curriculum theory was only taught in the former White English Universities together with their associated colleges of education, while White Afrikaans-medium and all other historically Black universities offered the now-defunct didactic tradition. This didactic tradition was intertwined with Fundamental Pedagogics and became the cornerstone of the apartheid education project. This explains why didactic tradition and fundamental became the object of populist scorn from those who were very critical of the overtly racist apart-heid education system (in particular, the Kenton conference education group-ing; Faatar, 2006).

This grouping had limited theoretical tools to engage with curriculum debates and worse so, in relation to race. This is despite the fact that they remain a potent, dominant force, influencing education policy direction in the post-apartheid South Africa (Faatar, 2006; Mafeje, 1998). Mafeje (ibid) contends that "black nationalists are administering an estate in which hege-mony belongs to the white liberals" (6). What is even more worrying is that these academics have a tendency of turning to class as a preferred category of sociological analysis while realities and continuing inequalities (observable) remain racialized (Mangcu, 2015). The project detailed here is an attempt to open up space for the robust theorization of education in relation to the interlocking systems of oppression, for example, race, gender and class. This is a deliberate attempt to cultivate agency for the decolonized HE. Decoloni-ality can aptly be summarized as a call for ontological turn in education and challenges us to reimagine theoretical frameworks that are "able to account for our lived experiences (as African people) and our relationality with other learners, (and a call to draw from) prisms rooted in our cultures, histories and heritage" (Dei, 2012, p. 1). Decolonial scholars unanimously call for the centrality of African ontological being (or endogeneity) in the academy and this is viewed as the prerequisite towards our struggles for epistemic free-dom (Mafeje, Magubane, Adesina, Nyoka, Ndlovu-Gatsheni and many more).

Following Mafeje (1998), we strongly believe that the only way to facilitate racial justice and truer emancipation of the Black oppressed people in South Africa is through Black Nationalism and African hegemony.

Graduate Attributes

While there is a wide range of literature around graduate attributes (GAs) in HE globally, there is unfortunately a lack of conceptual or theoretical clarity (Winberg et al., 2017). There is a tendency of linking GAs with expectations of the prospective employers, and in that way, university programmes are evaluated on to whether they meet such requirements (Griesel & Parker, 2009) and development of "wish lists" of skills to be added on (or embedded) in various university programmes. Winberg et al. (2017) cautioned against this "technical rationalism," and we continue to repudiate this tendency as we view it as akin to "selling out education," using the words of Allais (2003). At another level, we have some theorized versions of GAs even though left at an "imaginary level" or what Bhaskar would call "transcendental idealism" imagined world. However, we remain convinced that Capability Approach (CA) presents a very powerful way of capturing GAs with great potential to drive curriculum transformation agenda. In this project, we take CA beyond transcendental idealism through transcendental realism by developing GAs through CA with the aim of correcting the wrongs of past in HE. As Sayer noted,

> [i]t is recognized, of course, that enlightening people (or facilitating their own self-enlightenment) as to the source of the illusions and other unwanted determinations responsible for their plight is not a sufficient condition for their emancipation from them, and may indeed increase dissonance and despair: for emancipation, the mechanisms actually generating the problems must also be removed or blocked. It is important never to lose sight of the fact that the complex theories we develop to account for education and educational change are theories about the educational activities of people . . . [However] our theories will be about the educational activities of people even though they will not explain educational development strictly in terms of people alone.
>
> (1997, p. 7)

Bhaskar's diagram (Figure 8.1) illustrates our thinking and conceptual shifts around GAs: (1) It shows what we have called herein "technical rationality" or wish list and measurement exercise (outcomes-based education), (2) what we associate with the current development of GAs and (3) what we hope to achieve by developing GAs with the hope of correcting the wrongs of the past.

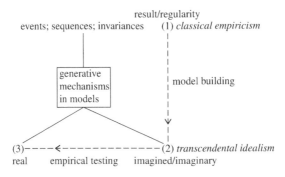

Figure 8.1 Bhaskar's transcendental realism

CA versus GAs

The genesis of CA is traced from the work of Amartya Sen (1997) and Martha Nussbaum (2001) and is very influential in international development. This work has also gained prominence in education (Bozalek, 2013; Walker & Boni, 2013; Unterhalter, 2009; Tikly & Barrett, 2007, and others). Simply put, capabilities are viewed as freedom, capacities and resources needed to make choices about how to live, while functionings can be viewed as the outcomes people achieve through using their capabilities.

Social analysis is needed to provide the social context for the development of capabilities and at the UoT, we have developed capabilities taking full consideration of the complexities of the postcolonial South Africa (our GAs speaks to this real reality). We were very much aware of the fact for capabilities (as potentials) would require us to engage and transform social relations for functionings to emerge.

Four capabilities were developed to achieve this end (see Figure 8.2):

1. Relational agency (working interculturally, linguistically and interprofessionally)

   Our graduate will be firmly rooted in African ontology (or Being) and understand our "relationality" with other cultures and social epistemologies. Central to this attribute is to acknowledge our colonial history and the importance of imagining life beyond the present.

2. Knowing and technological agency

   We took into cognizance the social reality of the merger and considered forms of knowledge and ways of knowing being valued in the

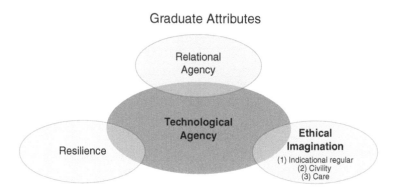

Figure 8.2 The Four Capabilities of Developing Graduate Attributes

post-merger South Africa University. We have taken the position that the GAs should be guided by issues of Science and Technology in Society. This also entails shifts and progression in ways in which we conduct our research project, which should move beyond the confinements of the closed systems (laboratories) and understand complexities of conducting research in open systems (society).

3. Ethics (personhood, societal and professional ethics)

We have included ethics as a basic social good and taking into consideration the cruelty and disrespect Black people had to endure during colonialism and apartheid.

4. Resilience ability (within research, innovation and entrepreneurial activities)

We believe that resilience is an important capability for students if these capabilities are to be achieved and functioning realized.

Conclusion

To round off, it is important to highlight the fact that we are fully aware of the challenges this curriculum transformation project is going to elicit. Critical realism provided a very solid meta-theoretical framework to guide the curriculum transformation project while enabling us to imagine society beyond the present. We needed to defend our sociological analysis and the category of social analysis due to the dominance of color-blind politics in the postcolonial South HE.

It is through CR that we could also engage with the possibility of reconstructing HE and GAs through CA, and we hope to contribute substantive frameworks to engage with racialized. We are hoping to draw the interest of scholars, students and academic leaders near and far in pursuit of our struggle for epistemic freedom for all.

Notes

1. *Decoloniality* here refers to a political and epistemological movement that seeks to fight against a global colonial system of White domination that continues to marginalize lives of Black people even after the demise of its formal juridical legislative framework. Decoloniality is direct response to coloniality and is viewed as a system that defines organization and dissemination of epistemic, moral and aesthetic resources in ways that mirror and reproduce modernity's imperial project (Andreotti, 2014: b).
2. Epistemic justice entails affirmation of ones being through equal participation (reciprocity) in the process of knowledge construction (Fricker, 2013).
3. Learning culture refers to social practices through which people learn. It does not mean learning context but implies exposure to discursive practices that condition human agency for curriculum change (James, 2014).
4. *Agency* here refers to radically transformed transformative praxis informed by our relative objective knowledge of the world.
5. This counterhegemonic curriculum entails challenging the status quo and the normative arrangement of the dominant Western ways of knowing, doing and being by presenting an alternative Black nationalism and African hegemony (Mafeje, 1998).
6. Intransitive world is independent of our minds. As human beings our knowledge of the world (transitive) keeps on changing as we want to account for this unknowable yet real world that conditions our life chances.

References

Allais, S. (2003). The national qualification framework in South Africa: A democratic project trapped in a neo-liberal paradigm. *Journal of Education and Work*, *16*(3), 305–324.

Andreotti, V. (2014). Conflicting epistemic demands in poststructuralist and postcolonial engagements with questions of complicity in systemic harm. *Educational Studies*, *50*(4), 378–397. doi:10.1080/00131946.2014.924940

Archer, A. (1979). *The social origins of educational systems*. London: Sage.

Archer, M. (1995). *Realist social theory: The morphogenetic approach*. Cambridge: Cambridge University Press.

Archer, M. (2003). *Structure, agency and the internal conversation*. Cambridge: Cambridge University Press.

Archer, M. (2007). *Making our way through the world: Human reflexivity and social mobility*. Cambridge: Cambridge University Press.

Badat, S. (2010). *The challenges of transformation in higher education and training institutions in South Africa*. South Africa: DBSA.

Badat, S. (2016). Deciphering the South African Higher Education Protests of 2015–16. Retrieved from. https://mellon.org/resources/shared-experiences-blog/south-africa-protests/

Bhaskar, R. (1978). *A realist theory of science*. Hassocks: Haverster Press.

Bhaskar, R. (1986). *Scientific Realism and Human Emancipation*. London: Verso.

Bonilla-Silva, E. (1997). Rethinking Racism: Toward a Structural Interpretation. *American Sociological Review, 62*(3), 465–480.

Bozalek, V. (2013). Equity and graduate attributes. In A. Boni & M. Walker (Ed). *Human development and capabilities: Re-imagining the university in the twenty-first century* (pp. 69–81). London: Routledge.

Cooper, David. (2015). Social Justice and South African University Student Enroll-ment Data by "Race," 1998–2012: From "Skewed Revolution" to "Stalled Revolution": SA Students from Skewed to Stalled Revolution. *Higher Education Quarterly*, 69. doi:10.1111/hequ.12074

Council on Higher Education (CHE). (2012). *VitalStats: Public Higher Education 2010*. Pretoria.

Council on Higher Education (CHE). (2013). *VitalStats: Public Higher Education 2011*. Pretoria.

Council on Higher Education (CHE). (2016). *South African Higher Education Reviewed: Two decades of Democracy*. Pretoria: South Africa. Retrieved from https://www.che.ac.za/sites/default/files/publications/CHE_South%20African%20 higher%20education%20reviewed%20-%20electronic.pdf

Dei, G. (2012). Indigenous anti-colonial knowledge as "heritage knowledge" for pro-moting Black/African education in diasporic contexts, *Decolonization: Indigeneity, Education & Society, 1*(1), 102–119.

Donati, P. (2016). The family as a source of relational goods (and Evils) for itself and for the community. *Italian Journal of Sociology of Education, 8*(3), 149–168.

Faatar, A. (2006). Policy networks in recalibrated political terrain: The case of school curriculum policy and politics in South Africa. *Journal of Education Policy, 21*(6), 641–659.

Fricker, M. (2013). Epistemic Justice as a Condition of Political Justice? *Synthese, 190*(7), 1317–1332. Retrieved from https://philpapers.org/rec/FRIEJA

Giroux, H.A. (2010). Bare pedagogy and the scourge of neoliberalism: Rethinking higher education as a democratic public sphere. *The Educational Forum, 74*(3), 184–196.

Griessel, H., & Parker, B. (2009). *Graduate attributes: A baseline study on South African graduates from the perspective of employers*. HESA & SAQA. Retrieved from http://www.cshe.uwc.ac.za/docs/2009/Graduate%20Attributes%20Report%20 -%20HESA.pdf

Hartwig, M. (ed). (2016). *Dictionary of Critical Realism*. London: Routledge.

James, D. (2014). Investigating the curriculum through assessment practice in higher education: The value of a "Leaning Cultures" Approach. *Higher Education, 67*(2), 155–169.

Kotta, L. (2008). *Knowledge, curriculum structures and identities in higher educa-tion*. Paper presented at the Higher Education Closeup 4 Conference, Cape Town.

Kraak, A., & Mahamed, N. (2001). Qualifications reform in higher education: An evaluation of the work of national standards bodies. In: M. Breirer (ed). *Curriculum restructuring in higher education in post-apartheid South Africa*. Education Policy Unit, University of the Western Cape.

Luckett, K. (2009). The relationship between knowledge structure and curriculum: A case study in sociology. *Studies in Higher Education, 34*(4), 441–453.

Mafeje, A. (1998). Anthropology and Independent Africans: Suicide or End of an Era?', *African Sociological Review, 2*(1), 1–43.

Mandani, M. (2004). *Good Muslims, Bad Muslims: America, the cold war, and the roots of terror.* Princeton, NJ: Random House.

Mangcu, X. (2015). *The colour of our future: Does race matter in post-apartheid South Africa*? Johannesburg: Wits University Press.

Maton, K. (2005). A question of autonomy: Bourdieu's field approach and higher education policy. *Journal of Education Policy, 20*(6), 687–704.

Maton, K. (2014). *Knowledge and knowers: Towards a realist sociology of education.* London: Routledge.

Mbembe, A. (2016). *Decolonizing Knowledge and the Question of the Archive.* Retrieved from http://wiser.wits.ac.za/system/files/Achille%20Mbembe%20-%20 Decolonizing%20Knowledge%20and%20the%20Question%20of%20the%20 Archive.pdf

Mills, C. (1997). *The racial contract.* Ithaca, NY: Cornell University Press.

Mills, C. (2015). *"Racial Equality" in The Equal Society: Essays on Equality in Theory and Practices.* George Hull (ed.). Lanham, MD: Lexington Books/Rowan and Littlefield.

Mills, C. (2017). *Black Rights/White Wrongs. The Critique of Racial Liberalism.* United States of America: Oxford University Press.

Muller, J. (2008). *In search of coherence: A conceptual guide to curriculum planning for comprehensive universities* (Report prepared for the SANTED project). Johannesburg: Centre for Education Policy Development.

Muller, J. (2009). Forms of knowledge and curriculum coherence. *Journal of Education and Work, 22*(3), 205–227.

Ndlovu-Gatsheni, S. (2018). The dynamics of epistemological decolonization in the 21st Century: Towards epistemic freedom. *Strategic Review for Southern Africa, 40*(1). Retrieved from https://www.up.ac.za/media/shared/85/Strategic%20 Review/vol%2040(1)/Ndlovu-Gatsheni.pdf

Nussbaum, M. (2001). *Upheavals of Thought: The Intelligence of Emotions.* Cambridge: University Press.

Sayer, A. (1997). Critical Realism and the limits to critical Social Science. *Journal for the Theory of Social Behaviour, 27*(4). Retrieved from https://pdfs.semanticscholar.org/a2fa/c21a771ab1c7edf0b9881ebec9ab749c44bc.pdf

Sen, A. (1997) Editorial: Human Capital and Human Capability. World Development, 25 (12), 1959–61.

Shay, S. (2013). Conceptualizing curriculum differentiation in higher education: A sociology of knowledge point of view. *British Journal of Sociology of Education, 34*(4), 563–582.

Shay, S. (2016). Decolonizing the curriculum: It's time for a strategy. The Conversation. https://theconversation.com/decolonising-thecurriculum-its-time-for-a-strategy-60598

Tikly, L., & Barrett, A. (2011). Social justice capabilities and quality of education in low income countries. *International Journal of Educational Development, 31.* doi:10.1016/j.ijedudev.2010.06.001.

Unterhalter, E. (2009). What is Equity in Education? Reflections from the Capability Approach. *Studies in Philosophy and Education, 28*(5), 415–424.

Van Manen, M. (1977). Linking ways of knowing with ways of being practical. *Curriculum Inquiry, 6*(3), 205–228.

Walker, M., & Boni, A. (eds). (2013). *Human Development and Capabilities. Re-Imagining the University of Twenty-first Century.* London and New York: Routledge Taylor and Francis Group.

Winberg, C. (2012, July 31). *Diplomas and degrees in professionally-orientated higher education.* Position paper prepared for the Cape Peninsula University of Technology Senate Academic Planning Committee.

Winberg, C., Staak, A., Bester, M., Sabata, S., Scholtz, D., Sebolao, R., Monnapula-Mapesela, M., Ronald, N., Makua, M., Snyman, J., & Machika, P. (2017). In search of graduate attributes: A survey of six flagship programmes. *South African Journal of Higher Education, 32.* doi:10.20853/32-1-1642

Contributors

Eunice N. Ivala is an Associate Professor and Coordinator Educational Technology at the Centre for Innovative Educational Technology at Cape Peninsula University of Technology (CPUT) located in Cape Town, South Africa. Her research focus is on information and communication technology (ICT)–mediated teaching and learning in developing contexts. She has published/co-published more than 60 research papers and co-edited/edited two conference proceedings and one book. In 2018, she won an award for excellence in e-Learning from Global Learn Tech for her research impact in changing educational and individuals' practices. Recently, she was a team member in an international digital storytelling project dealing with foreign youth experiences abroad, which was supported by the European Union; a team leader of the ICT curriculum appraisal of the National Senior Certificate for Adults; and an institutional coordinator for the Council for Higher Education quality enhancement project in the area of learning environments; and she was a team member in a National Research Fund–British Council Workshop Links project on widening access, success and employability, a collaboration between CPUT and the University of East London, UK. She holds a BEd Honours degree from the University of Nairobi, Kenya; a MEd degree in Computer-based Education from the University of Natal, Durban, South Africa; and a PhD in Culture, Communication and Media Studies from the University of KwaZulu Natal, Durban, South Africa.

Chaunda L. Scott earned a doctorate in Organizational Leadership with a focus in diversity education from Teachers College/Columbia University in New York City, New York, USA, and a Master of Education degree in the area of Administration, Planning and Social Policy from the Harvard Graduate School of Education in Cambridge, Massachusetts, USA. She is currently an Associate Professor in the Department of Organizational Leadership in the School of Education and Human Services at Oakland University in Rochester, Michigan, USA, and Coordinator of the Graduate Human Diversity

Inclusion and Social Justice Interdisciplinary Certificate Programme. She also serves as the Diversity and Inclusion Specialist for the Office of the Dean in the school. In addition to the preceding, in 2018, Dr. Scott was selected by the Office of Academic Affairs at Oakland University for a prestigious Special Diversity Assignment.

In the Department of Organizational Leadership, she teaches undergraduate and graduate courses focused on the areas of workforce diversity, human resource development, organizational leadership and training and development. Additionally, she supervises diversity and social justice focused dissertations. In the area of scholarship, Dr. Scott has published several national and international diversity education and workforce diversity scholarly articles, book chapters, a book review and four co-edited workforce diversity books. She is also a recipient of an Academy of Human Resource Development's prominent Cutting Edge Research Award, and she has been named as one of the Top 25 Education Professors in Michigan by Online Schools.

Most notable in 2015, she was granted a prestigious Fulbright Specialist Award that took her to Cape Town, South Africa, where she provided professional development seminars at Cape Peninsula University of Technology to administrators and faculty in areas of diversity curriculum and program development. She also received the Educator of the Year Award in 2015 from the Niagara Foundation – Michigan Chapter for her exemplary diversity education work at Oakland University. In 2018, Dr. Scott was recognized at the 23rd Annual Oakland University Faculty Recognition Luncheon for her highly regarded and cutting-edge workforce diversity scholarship.

Johannes Cronjé is Dean of the Faculty of Informatics and Design at the Cape Peninsula University of Technology. He started his career as a schoolmaster at Pretoria Boys High School, then became a lecturer in communication at Pretoria Technikon, and later a professor of Computers in Education at the University of Pretoria.

He holds two masters' degrees and a doctorate from the University of Pretoria and was visiting professor at universities in Norway, Finland, Sudan, Ethiopia and Belgium. He has supervised more than 75 master's and 80 doctoral students and has published more than 45 academic articles and chapters in books. He holds a C1 rating from the South African National Research Foundation. His research interests focus on how people learn from one another using technology. In particular, his research and postgraduate supervision over the last few years have concentrated on how Web 3.0 technologies have caused a paradigm shift in the focus of learning from the individual to the system. As such his interest lies in the "Rhizomatic" nature of learning that has become increasingly facilitated by mobile learning. Recommender systems form an integral part of such learning as they both depend on and contribute to the rhizomatic learning system.

In 2008 he won the African ICT Achiever award in the category Teaching and Learning, and in 2015 he was a visiting scholar at the KU Leuven on an Erasmus Mundus scholarship.

He is married to Franci, and they have three children, two dogs and two cats.

Xena Cupido is Academic Development Senior Lecturer at the Cape Peninsula University of Technology. She works in the Academic Staff Development Unit in Fundani: Centre for Higher Education Development. Her responsibilities include the coordination and implementation of the student feedback on teaching and courses project for the institution. She is one of the 2018 TAU (Teaching Advancement at University) Fellows and a committee member of the Higher Education Learning and Teaching Association of Southern Africa Tutor and Mentor Special Interest Group. Xena Cupido holds a PhD in Educational Psychology. Her research interest includes socially just pedagogies, student engagement and support as well as community engagement.

Daniela Gachago is an Associate Professor in the Centre for Innovative Educational Technology at the Cape Peninsula University of Technology. She has more than 15 years of experience in academic staff development and training in innovative teaching and learning practices across the world. Originally from Austria she has lived in South Africa since 2010. Her research interests lie in the potential of emerging technologies to transform teaching and learning in higher education. More and more she has been drawn to issues of social justice in education, such as the ethics of blended and open learning in contexts of inequality and multimodal pedagogies such as digital storytelling as decolonial classroom practices. She believes in the power of storytelling not only to learn more about oneself but also to learn about the other and allow collective narratives to emerge. She has been using digital storytelling for many years across different disciplines and contexts to engage students and lecturers in difficult conversations around identity, race, gender or class. She sees herself as a critical pedagogue concerned with developing critical thinkers in her teaching practice. She holds a master's degree in Adult Education from the University of Botswana and a PhD in Education from the University of Cape Town.

Jolanda Morkel is a registered architect and senior lecturer in the Department of Architectural Technology and Interior Design at the Cape Peninsula University of Technology in Cape Town, South Africa. She has taught across all levels of the diploma and bachelor's degree (BTech) in Architectural Technology, and designed, coordinated and facilitated various transformative learning and teaching innovations. These include the first interdisciplinary extended curriculum programme focused on the spatial design disciplines (architecture and interior design) and blended and flexible work integrated and vocational learning models at the Diploma and BTech levels, serving culturally diverse and non-traditional students.

Jolanda's research interests related to learning and teaching include flexible and blended learning, technology-mediated, service learning and work-integrated learning experiences and learning design. Her doctoral research, under the supervision of Prof J. C. Cronjé, explores the student–tutor interaction in the live online architectural design critique. She regularly publishes, presents at conferences and enjoys sketch noting and facilitating workshops on learning design.

Alex Noble is a Lecturer at the Cape Peninsula University of Technology. She is the Programme Leader for Architectural Technology in the Department of Architectural Technology and Interior Design as well as the extended curriculum programme (ECP) year coordinator for Architectural Technology. Alex has recently registered for her PhD through the University of the Western Cape in the Department of Education and Post-School studies. Her PhD research focus is on socially just pedagogies in Architectural Technology ECP.

Najwa Norodien-Fataar is acting Head of Department of the Student Learning Unit in the Fundani Centre for Higher Education Development at the Cape Peninsula University of Technology. She holds a doctorate in Education from Stellenbosch University. She is a lecturer in academic development and coordinates and trains senior students and postgraduate students for the tutor and teaching assistant programme at the university's District Six campus. Her previous positions include an academic development lecturer in the Economics and Management Sciences Faculty, Faculty of Community and Health Sciences and Faculty of Education at the University of Western Cape. She has published extensively in the areas of student learning and engagement, first-generation students, student access and support and information and communication technology in higher education. She is a member of the Higher Education Learning and Teaching Association of Southern Africa Special Interest Group for Tutoring and Mentoring and a member of the South African Education Research Association.

Monwabisi K. Ralarala is an Associate Professor and Director: Fundani Centre for Higher Education Development at the Cape Peninsula University of Technology. He also holds the position of Chairperson: African Language

Association of South Africa. His previous positions include Director: Language Centre (University of Fort Hare), Institutional Language Coordinator (Cape Peninsula University of Technology), Chairperson of the Western Cape Language Committee, Director of Research and Policy Development (Commission for the Promotion and Protection of the Rights of Cultural, Religious and Linguistic Communities) and Lecturer at the University of Stellenbosch's Department of African Languages. Apart from being a Canon Collins Educational and Legal Assistance Trust Alumnus, Monwabisi is the 2017 recipient of the Neville Alexander Award for the Promotion of Multilingualism. Monwabisi holds two PhDs (Universities of Stellenbosch and Free State, respectively) in persuasion in African Languages and in Language Practice (emphasis in forensic linguistics). His research interests are quite diverse but follow three lines: language rights and multilingualism in higher education, forensic linguistics and translation studies. Monwabisi has held visiting scholarships abroad for purposes of teaching and research (Leipzig, Germany and Purdue, US). He has also published articles and book chapters mainly in forensic linguistics and translation studies. His recent (2017) co-edited book is titled *African Language and Language Practice Research in the 21st Century: Interdisciplinary Themes and Perspectives* (CASAS).

Siya Sabata is a lecturer responsible for the development of graduate attributes (GAs) and curriculum transformation in the Curriculum Development Unit within Fundani Centre for Higher Education Development at the Cape Peninsula University of Technology (CPUT). He is the co-founder and leader of CPUT curriculum decoloniality group which is using the GAs project as a mechanism to drive curriculum decolonial agenda. He is also teaching in a Post Graduate Diploma in Higher Education, a collaborative programme offered jointly with the University of Stellenbosch and the University of the Western Cape. Siya is a critical realist scholar inspired by the philosophy of the late Roy Bhaskar and works in the field of academic staff development. His scholarship draws on the tradition of sociology of education, in particular the trend of social realism developed by Karl Maton, in his Legitimation Code Theory (LCT). He is currently developing linkages between LCT and *The Racial Contract*, the work of Charles. W. Mills to strengthen the theoretical language of description necessary to engage with social practices in a racialised context. Siya served in the executive committee of Higher Education Learning and Teaching Association of Southern Africa (HELTASA, 2013–2014). He also participated in the Review of South African Higher Education, Two decades of democracy, in 2016. Siya holds MPhil: Social Policy from the University of Cape Town and is currently writing his PhD at Rhodes University, where he is interrogating social construction of the teacher education pedagogic discourse.

Zilungile Sosibo is an Associate Professor of Education in the Faculty of Education at Cape Peninsula University of Technology. She is also Head of Department of the Senior Phase and Further Education and Training (SP&FET) Department. Her research focus is mainly on Assessment and Evaluation and Diversity and Transformation in Higher Education. She has published extensively in both areas. Over the years she has obtained several grants, including the National Research Foundation (NRF)-Knowledge, Interchange and Collaboration grants in 2016 and 2018, the NRF Competitive Grants for Unrated researchers (2014–2016 & 2017–2019) and several other grants from CPUT. Recently, she has successfully hosted the 2018 45th International Conference of the Southern African Society of Education which took place on 3–5 October 2018 in Cape Town, South Africa. She also boasts several partnerships which extend beyond the South African borders. She has served on a number of councils, including Umalusi Council (2006–2014), The Council on Higher Education (2011–2015) and Northlink College Council (2009–2011).

Kristian Stewart is a King Chavez Park Faculty Fellow and University of Michigan Diversity Scholar at the University of Michigan in Dearborn, Michigan, USA. Her scholarship centers on digital storytelling, and she conducts research on its implications in literacy, decolonizing/anti-racist curriculum and as a humanizing pedagogical practice. Dr. Stewart recently finished a grant-related work stemming from the Flint (MI) water crisis.

Index

Page numbers in italics indicate figures and in bold indicate tables on the corresponding pages.

134   *Index*

136   *Index*

Taylor & Francis eBooks

www.taylorfrancis.com

A single destination for eBooks from Taylor & Francis
with increased functionality and an improved user
experience to meet the needs of our customers.

90,000+ eBooks of award-winning academic content in
Humanities, Social Science, Science, Technology, Engineering,
and Medical written by a global network of editors and authors.

TAYLOR & FRANCIS EBOOKS OFFERS:

A streamlined
experience for
our library
customers

A single point
of discovery
for all of our
eBook content

Improved
search and
discovery of
content at both
book and
chapter level

REQUEST A FREE TRIAL
support@taylorfrancis.com

 Routledge
Taylor & Francis Group

 CRC Press
Taylor & Francis Group

For Product Safety Concerns and Information please contact our
EU representative GPSR@taylorandfrancis.com Taylor & Francis
Verlag GmbH, Kaufingerstraße 24, 80331 München, Germany